CAMBRIDGE STUDIES IN LATIN AMERICAN
AND IBERIAN LITERATURE 8

Journalism and the development of Spanish American narrative

The relationship between literature and journalism is an important element in the literary history of all Spanish America. The very first Spanish American novelist, the Mexican José Joaquín Fernández de Lizardi, was a journalist, and virtually all Spanish American writers, from Sarmiento through Martí, to Borges and García Márquez, have, at one time or another, been involved in journalism. This book explores the impact of journalism and journalistic rhetoric on the development of Spanish American narrative, from its beginnings in the early nineteenth century to the testimonial and documentary novels of contemporary authors, such as Miguel Barnet and Elena Poniatowska. González examines selected works from the Spanish American narrative tradition that exemplify moments in the history of the relationship between literature and journalism. He argues that Spanish-American narrative has sought to work in consonance with journalism's modernizing impulse, making strategic use of journalistic discourse to promote social or political change. In the course of the argument, González offers a broad historical panorama of the journalism–narrative interaction, and at the same time proposes an alternate theory of the development of the Spanish American narrative.

CAMBRIDGE STUDIES IN LATIN AMERICAN AND IBERIAN LITERATURE

Journalism and the development of Spanish American narrative

ANÍBAL GONZÁLEZ
Michigan State University

CAMBRIDGE
UNIVERSITY PRESS

CAMBRIDGE UNIVERSITY PRESS
Cambridge, New York, Melbourne, Madrid, Cape Town, Singapore, São Paulo

Cambridge University Press
The Edinburgh Building, Cambridge CB2 2RU, UK

Published in the United States of America by Cambridge University Press, New York

www.cambridge.org
Information on this title: www.cambridge.org/9780521414258

First published 1993
This digitally printed first paperback version 2006

A catalogue record for this publication is available from the British Library

Library of Congress Cataloguing in Publication data
González, Aníbal.
Journalism and the development of Spanish American narrative /
Aníbal González.
p.   cm. – (Cambridge studies in Latin American and Iberian
literature ; 8)
Includes bibliographical references and index.
ISBN 0–521–41425–3
1. Spanish American fiction – History and criticism.   2. Journalism
and literature – Latin America.   I. Title.   II. Series.
PQ7082.N7G66   1993
863–dc20   92–45568
                                                                  CIP

ISBN-13 978-0-521-41425-8 hardback
ISBN-10 0-521-41425-3 hardback

ISBN-13 978-0-521-02735-9 paperback
ISBN-10 0-521-02735-7 paperback

To my father,
Aníbal González Irizarry,
on his 45th anniversary in broadcast
journalism

Contents

Acknowledgments

This book is an extension – by no means a culmination – of my longstanding interest in the parallel histories of journalism and narrative fiction in Spanish America. It is an interest linked to my personal background: my father, Aníbal González Irizarry, is a broadcast journalist, a news anchorman. Some of my earliest memories of what Derrida would call the "scene of writing" are of seeing my father at work in his office in the Puerto Rican TV network Telemundo (WKAQ-Channel 2), composing the reports he would read daily on-camera, as well as editing and translating the news that came over the teletypes.

Clearly, a discussion of the origins of this text could easily lead me into autobiography, a genre I enjoy reading but try to avoid writing. But a book such as this is also the end result of numerous readings, conversations, and consultations over the years, the residue of a textual as well as spoken dialogue with friends, colleagues, and total strangers near and far. Unlike journalists, who jealously guard their sources, scholars must publicly acknowledge them, and I do so with immense gratitude. The vast majority of those who have helped me in this enterprise are recognized in the notes and bibliography, but I would like to single out here a handful who may not have received their due in the pages that follow. First, I am grateful to my good friends Houchang Chehabi, of Harvard, and Frieda Brown, of Michigan State University, both of whom cheerfully volunteered for the thankless task of reading this work in manuscript form, and who helped purge it of many errors and infelicities (for those that remain they are blameless, of course). I would also like to thank Gustavo Pérez-Firmat, whose sensible suggestions about style and organization helped me bring my text into greater focus. I am grateful for the unfailing encouragement of Enrique Pupo-Walker, the general editor of this series. Among the many friends with whom I have shared ideas about the subject of this book, I wish to single out particularly for their help Carlos J. Alonso, Arturo Echavarría, Alfredo Bryce Echenique, Cathy L. Jrade, Sylvia Molloy, and Kathleen Ross. My gratitude goes also to my former doctoral students, now esteemed colleagues in the profession: Peter Elmore, César Ferreira, Cristóbal Pera, Carlos Figueras, and Jorge Marcone, who at various times listened patiently to my monologues and offered welcome advice. Last but never least, my wife and colleague Priscilla Meléndez has been both a keen-eyed reader of this book and my most constant supporter. I am forever indebted to her intelligence and her love.

1

Journalism, modernity, and narrative fiction in Spanish America

We are more concerned . . . with the question of whether a history of an entity as self-contradictory as literature is conceivable. In the present state of literary studies this possibility is far from being clearly established. It is generally admitted that a positivistic history of literature, treating it as if it were a collection of empirical data, can only be a history of what literature is not. . . . On the other hand, the intrinsic interpretation of literature claims to be anti- or ahistorical, but often presupposes a notion of history of which the critic is not himself aware.

Paul de Man, "Literary History and Literary Modernity"

Which of us is writing this page I don't know.

Jorge Luis Borges, "Borges and I"

In the heady days of the student protests that led to the massacre at Tiananmen Square in China in 1989, a telling indication of how much circumstances seemed to be changing in the direction the student leaders wanted was the sudden lifting of curbs on the press, as Chinese print and electronic journalists were for the first time able to report with considerable freedom on the social upheaval.[1] Such freedom was promptly crushed, as was the student uprising, but its brief flowering, in the midst of a student-led rebellion demanding that China's modernization be sociopolitical as well as economic, served as a reminder of journalism's deep and perennial link to modernity.

To all Spanish Americans, particularly to Mexicans and those familiar with Mexico, the Tiananmen repression must have brought back ironic memories of a similar event: the 1968 Tlatelolco massacre, when hundreds of people demonstrating for greater freedom of expression were gunned down in the

Plaza of the Three Cultures in central Mexico City. The irony
in those memories must surely come from the fact that, whereas the Chinese protests were broadcast live via satellite around
the world, the events at Tlatelolco went almost unreported at
the time by the government-coopted Mexican press. The ab-
sence of the media at the Tlatelolco events was as significant as
their presence at the Chinese events. The lack of reporting by
the media prompted an impassioned response by Mexican writers, and soon essays, poems, and testimonial narratives by
such authors as Octavio Paz, José Emilio Pacheco, Rosario Castellanos, and Elena Poniatowska poured forth to investigate,
denounce, and reflect on the tragedy. If Tiananmen reminds
us of the abiding connection between journalism and modernity, Tlatelolco and its aftermath underscore the unique intensity
and volatility of the relationships among modernity, nationhood, journalism, and literature in Spanish America.

The concept of "modernity" is a complex and highly charged
one that has been much debated of late, particularly in regard
to the possible existence of a "postmodernity." For my purposes, I regard modernity as both a definite historical period
and an all-encompassing cultural phenomenon. First of all,
modernity is the name given to the profound socioeconomic,
political, cultural, and technological changes that began in
Western Europe at the end of the eighteenth century and have
subsequently been disseminated over much of the world. As a
sociohistorical concept it encompasses, among other things,
capitalism and its discontents, representative government, and
a belief in the transformative power of technology. But it also
implies a deep cultural shift with regard to previous modes of
being: In the cultural sphere, modernity is linked to change, to
renewal, to the twin ideas of progress and decadence, to historicism, to criticism, and to the presumed provisional character of
all socioeconomic and political structures.[2]

I furthermore agree with those who have argued that Spanish America – as a political and cultural ideal, if not as an
accomplished fact – is both a source and a product of modernity.[3] The key role played by the New World in the origins of the
modern age in Europe has already been amply documented;
less recognized is the fact that the struggle for Spanish America's independence in the early nineteenth century was an at-

tempt by the Creole elites to bring modernity to their native lands. Literary works as diverse as Andrés Bello's *Silva a la agricultura de la zona tórrida* (1823) and Domingo Faustino Sarmiento's *Facundo, o Civilización y barbarie* (1854) attest that the Creoles' nation-building during the independence period was intended to bring Spanish America in line with the letter – if not always the spirit – of modernity.

A product of the modern age, Spanish America has always had a problematical relation to modernity. Throughout the nineteenth century, the modern spirit of the incipient Spanish American bourgeoisie came face to face with an archaic and threatening reality that was usually represented in Romantic texts by the forces of Nature – impenetrable jungles, endless plains – but which in fact was only the legacy of the systems of production of the Colonial period.[4] From the time of the wars of independence the young Creole bourgeoisie, although anxious to reproduce upon American soil the ideological, aesthetic, and economic novelties of Europe, was faced with the question of what to do with the great masses of Indians, peons, and slaves, who were barely acculturated and lacked the necessary training to perform the complicated tasks of the new industries. Unwilling to regard these people as their countrymen and to grant them even a few basic freedoms, the Creoles were unable to transform them into the disciplined, docile, and educated work force needed to fuel an industrial revolution. Against this background occurred the struggles of Simón Bolívar against the plainsmen of Boves, the conflict between Unitarians and Federalists in Argentina, and the desperate tug-of-war of the Cuban sugar barons with the very system of slave labor on which their sugar mills depended.[5] It was, broadly speaking, the struggle of "civilization" against a "barbarism" on which the former ultimately depended, and which it must exploit like just another natural resource in order to survive.[6] Spanish American modernity appears, then, as the product of a will to power, of a violence that must be exerted and renewed periodically upon a milieu that actively or passively rejects it.

The violence exerted by modernity was, at least in part, that of the pen. Following an age-old Western tradition, the Spanish American ruling class adopted representation – particularly written representation – as an important weapon in its arsenal.

However, unable to successfully transplant modern systems of production, the Spanish American elite instead imported new modes of representation, naively hoping to find the solution to its problems in the critical spirit fostered by the latter. Thus, throughout the nineteenth century there arose a succession of discourses that dealt not so much with the question of the existence of a Spanish American modernity as with the possibility of its actualization in Spanish America. One of these discourses was that of historiography and political analysis, embodied in wide-ranging works of Romantic erudition such as Lucas Alamán's *Disertaciones sobre la historia de México* (1844–52) and the Cuban José Antonio Saco's *Historia de la esclavitud* (1875–92). Another was what we may broadly call "literature": This category includes a variety of works which obliquely reflected the modernizing project, from the patriotic odes of the independence period that constituted, in Rubén Darío's dyspeptic judgment, "an eternal song to Junín, an unending ode to the agriculture of the torrid zone" (*Obras completas,* I: 206), to profoundly meditated and anguished texts such as Esteban Echeverría's "El matadero" (written in 1839, but published in 1871), Sarmiento's *Facundo,* and Cirilo Villaverde's *Cecilia Valdés* (1879). Still another discourse, certainly not the least important, was that of journalism, embodied in the myriad ephemeral publications (broadsheets, pamphlets, journals, dailies) that proliferated after independence and in some cases went on to become, later in the nineteenth century, powerful shapers of public opinion.

Since I will be speaking throughout the rest of this book about the two discourses of literature and journalism, some definitions are in order. With regard to literature, I agree with Tzvetan Todorov's view that the attempt to define it as a specific type of discourse is a questionable enterprise (*The Poetics of Prose,* p. 1). Todorov prefers to dissolve "the opposition between literature and nonliterature" into "a typology of discourses" (p. 11). Nevertheless, ever since its inception in the nineteenth century, "literature" is a notion which has refused to disappear. It is clearly a term that encapsulates certain ideals of textual production deeply rooted in modern writers, most notably those of linguistic autonomy and self-referentiality – what Foucault has called the "radical intransitivity" of language (*Les mots et les choses*, p. 313) – and the vision of the writer as an intellectual aristocrat (Kernan, "The Idea of Literature," p. 38–9). Although I share Todorov's basic belief that "literature" is a historically determined concept and that "discourse" is a more useful category with which to reflect on textual phenomena (p. 11), I will occasionally invoke the former term, particularly as my analysis draws closer to our era, because texts written in more recent times often presuppose literature's existence as part of their textual ideology.

And what do I mean by "journalism"? Similar caveats apply to this concept, with one distinction: In my view, unlike literature, journalism's use of language has been sufficiently formalized and regulated throughout history to warrant considering journalism a type of discourse, albeit one that has been substantially reformulated over the years (I have more to say about this later in this chapter). The term "journalism" is used today to refer in general to "the activity of gathering and disseminating news" (Stephens, p. 3n), but it was not used in its current sense until the late eighteenth century,[7] and the forms this activity has taken have historically been quite diverse: letters, newsbooks, news ballads, gazettes, etc. The very notion of "news" is subject to debate. For instance, what is "new" in "news"? When does "news" begin to shade off into history? In eighteenth-century England, the Stamp Act, which attempted to tax newspapers, led eventually to a pragmatic, legal definition of "news" as "a narrative of public events supplied by the posts and under one month old" (Davis, p. 99). Obviously, such arbitrary deadlines do little to solve the underlying philosophical problem of time: how to define the present. Nevertheless, however "the present" is understood, terms such as "journalism" or "the press," like the term "literature," have clearly come to encompass certain ideals of textual production. In the case of journalism, these ideals are constantly evolving and have often been in opposition to those of literature: Specifically, journalism insists on language's utilitarian aspect – particularly its subordination to the laws of the market, to money – and on language's transitivity, its transparency as a medium through which information is conveyed as objectively as possible. Needless to say, the journalistic ideal of linguistic transparency and objectivity has often been contradicted by journalism's use as a vehicle for propaganda and polemic. This has been particularly true in Spanish America, and is an important element in the definition of "journalism" in that particular context, as will be seen later in this chapter.

I wish to make clear from the outset that although I sometimes refer to the relationship between literature and journalism in terms of an antagonism or an opposition, I am using such binary distinctions as shorthand for a far more complex situation. In the lexicon of chaos theory (which seems particularly germane in this case, see below), I view both literature and journalism as dynamic systems in which other dynamic systems such as writing, commerce, philosophy, and art come together. The same can be said of various categories and generic terms I use throughout this study, such as "narrative," "narrative fiction," "novel," "short story," etc., including the concept of "discourse" itself. All these terms must be construed, in the abysmatic perspective afforded by chaos theory, as ephemeral vortices of signification made up of other vortices. Nevertheless, their unstable, sometimes provisional character does not make them less real or effective: To use a meteorological metaphor, a tornado or a thunderstorm is no less real for being an ephemeral phenomenon. What I propose in this study is a still-crude model of textuality which will hopefully help to answer certain questions, such as: Why have so many Spanish American authors been journalists (as many still are)? Is this situation unusual? Has this had any effect on the various genres of narrative prose in Spanish America, particularly on the novel? Are the allusions to journalism in so many well-known works of Spanish American narrative fiction significant in this regard? And how? I believe the persistence of these questions among critics of Spanish American literature indicates that a relationship of some sort has existed and continues to exist between those two complex phenomena: narrative fiction (some of which is "literary" in today's terms) and journalism.

Indeed, the link between narrative fiction and journalism is a well-known but little-researched area of Spanish American literary history. This relationship is not exclusive to Spanish America, of course; it is an important element in the literary history of all Western nations, and has been studied, with varying methodologies and degrees of success, with regard to En-

glish, French, U.S., and Spanish literature.[8] Nevertheless, satis-
factory theoretical works are still lacking on the general
literary–historical problem of the interaction between narrative fiction and journalism. Furthermore, aside from scattered
but valuable works on such topics as the Spanish American
testimonial and documentary narratives, the journalism of Carpentier, García Márquez, and Donoso, and the Modernist
newspaper chronicles, no substantial book-length studies have
been done on this subject in Spanish America.[9]

As one begins to approach this unusually complex field,
three basic theoretical and methodological questions come to
mind. First, are there any intrinsic differences between journalism and narrative fiction? Second, if there are, what detectable
traces has journalism left in narrative fiction throughout history? And, last, why do fiction writers make use of journalistic
discourse and its devices? Needless to say, these questions have
no simple answer, and I can only begin to propose some working hypotheses.

In my approach, I use (as noted above) certain terms and
concepts advisedly. One such term is "discourse," which I use
not so much in Emile Benveniste's rather general linguistic definition ("any speech-act supposing a speaker and a listener, and
in the speaker an intention to influence the listener in some
way," pp. 208–9) but in a more idiosyncratic usage that derives
from Michel Foucault as well as from his critics and commenta-
tors such as Hayden White. First and foremost, "discourse" is a
broad-ranging category that encompasses the myriad ways in
which human language organizes knowledge. Foucault coined
this usage because of his distrust, as Mark Philp notes, of "the
traditional units of analysis and interpretation – text, oeuvre,
and genre – as well as the postulated unities in science – theories, paradigms, and research programmes" (p. 69). "Discourse" is also a concept that moves, that shuttles back and forth
(as is suggested by the word's Latin root, *discurrere*) between
other concepts, helping to critically dissolve some and to bring
others together. As Hayden White points out,

A discourse moves "to and fro" between received encodations of experience and the clutter of phenomena which refuses incorporation
into conventionalized notions of "reality," "truth," or "possibility." It
also moves "back and forth" (like a shuttle?) between alternative ways

of encoding this reality, some of which may be provided by the traditions of discourse prevailing in a given domain of inquiry and others of which may be idiolects of the author, the authority of which he is seeking to establish. Discourse, in a word, is quintessentially a *mediative* enterprise. As such, it is both interpretive and preinterpretive; it is always as much *about* the nature of interpretation itself as it is *about* the subject matter which is the manifest occasion of its own elaboration. (p. 4; italics in original)

Discourse almost never appears in a "pure" and solitary state (save, perhaps, as Foucault suggests, in the speech of madmen [*Histoire de la folie,* p. 39]); instead, it usually appears already subject to the controls and sanctions of society, which considers its free manifestations suspect. "In any society," Foucault proposes in *L'ordre du discours,* "the production of discourse is at once controlled, selected, organized and redistributed according to a number of procedures whose role is to avert its powers and its dangers, to master the unpredictable event . . ." (pp. 10–11). That is why "discourse," when used as a noun, frequently bears an adjective in front of it, as in the terms "literary discourse" or "journalistic discourse."

One of the ways in which society seeks to control discourse is by using it as a tool to affect the real world – by turning it into practice, so to speak. Foucault frequently speaks of "discursive formations," specific discourses that serve as models for real-world institutions (such as hospitals, prisons, churches; or universities) that in turn attempt to regulate human thought and action in terms of the discourses they represent. Needless to say, literature and journalism have not escaped such a process of institutionalization. Throughout the nineteenth century, in salons, cenacles, schools, and "movements," there was a tendency to gather a multiplicity of textual productions and to standardize certain types of writing under the rubric of "literature," thus turning literature into a sort of "protodiscourse." For very different reasons having to do with that activity's commercial aspect, journalism was also being institutionalized, and with much greater success, to the extent that it truly developed into a discourse – that is, a set of rules governing the display of information. Literature and journalism are both ways in which discourse has been, to a certain extent, mastered and controlled, although clearly literature has managed to preserve its unruly and unpredictable nature to a far greater extent than journalism.[10]

Returning to my first question, it is difficult to say whether there is an intrinsic difference between literature and journalistic discourse. Perhaps it would be better to say that *difference* is at the heart of the link between literature and journalism. A dialectic of difference and resemblance runs through the history of both discourses. For simplicity's sake, I will use narrative fiction as an instance of "literature," although I realize it does not always fit that category. Let us first briefly enumerate the resemblances:

(1) From a socioliterary standpoint, both journalism and narrative fiction in its most common modern forms – the novel and the short story – are linked to the rise of the bourgeoisie and to the bourgeois insistence on keeping account of facts as well as profits.[11]

(2) It is noteworthy that from its beginnings in the early gazettes and journals of late-sixteenth-century Europe, journalistic discourse has adopted or adapted a whole range of genres – letters, dialogues, diaries, *relaciones*, and so forth – which also fall within the purview of narrative fiction. Narrative fiction itself is persistently (some would say, perversely) mimetic, constantly imitating other discourses; thus, we have novels posing as histories, diaries, letters, or journalistic reportages.

(3) From an ideological perspective, journalism and narrative fiction share the philosophical problematics of empiricism. As Ian Watt has shown, the early picaresque novels and Cervantes' *Quijote* foreshadowed the problematics of empiricism that was later expounded systematically in Locke's *Essay Concerning Human Understanding* and was subsequently taken up by English and French novelists (pp. 9–34). Empiricism is also the hallmark of journalistic discourse, with its insistence on facts over fiction, on information over narration.

(4) Finally, at the level of rhetoric, Roland Barthes' observations on the presumed difference between historical and fictive discourse are applicable to journalism as well, insofar as journalism attempts to write a "history of the present":

The only feature which distinguishes historical discourse from other kinds is a paradox: the "fact" can exist linguistically only as a term in a discourse, yet we behave as if it were a simple reproduction of something on another plane of existence altogether, some extra-structural "reality." Historical discourse is presumably the only kind which aims at a referent "outside" itself that can in fact never be reached. . . . [It is therefore a] fake performative, in which what claims to be the descriptive element is in fact only the expression of the authoritarian nature of that particular speech-act. ("Le discours de l'histoire," pp. 73, 74)

Both narrative fiction and journalism thrive in a murky rhetorical frontier, an ill-defined territory of mutual borrowings where nothing is quite what it seems. The interaction between them may be more clearly visualized by referring to Jorge Luis Borges' parable "Borges and I" (1960), in which he evokes the metaphor of the hourglass to represent the process whereby his inner self (the narrative's "I") "pours" itself into the literary persona known as "Borges." However, in its final line ("Which of us is writing this page, I don't know," p. 70) the text presents its readers with a conundrum: To which entity do we assign the text we are reading? Since it has already been written, do we simply assign it to "Borges," the narrator's literary persona? But, since the narrator stresses the act of writing and the confessional, intimate nature of his discourse, doesn't the text properly belong to the inner self? Clearly, "Borges and I" exists in a dynamic, shifting region, like the hourglass's narrow waist, in which it is impossible to say whether the process has ended or still goes on. In a similar fashion, narrative fiction and journalism transfer into their respective spheres elements from each other's domain; the domains themselves are not difficult to differentiate, but the textual products of their interaction are harder to separate.

Nevertheless, unlike Borges' hourglass metaphor, which suggests that the discourse of the self "flows" unidirectionally toward that of the literary persona, the situation of narrative fiction and journalism is more complex, since there is a constant back-and-forth movement of elements between both discourses. A less literary but perhaps more precise way to view this situation would be to describe it, in the jargon of chaos theory, as a nonlinear system, that is, as a textual analogue to apparently random, natural, and everyday phenomena such as the weather, the ups and downs of the stock market, the dripping of water from a faucet, or the unpredictable movements of a double-jointed pendulum.[12] The latter phenomenon, as explained by N. Katherine Hayles, is a particularly lucid illustration of nonlinearity:

> Imagine a normal pendulum, with one end fixed and one end swinging free. When the amplitude of oscillation is small, its motion can be modeled using linear differential equations. Now suppose that we fasten a second pendulum at the swinging end of the first pendulum, so that the structure becomes double-jointed, as it were. Although the double pendulum follows Newtonian laws of motion as rigorously as a simple pendulum, the evolution of the double-jointed system cannot be predicted. Moreover, over a wide range of energies, its motion cannot adequately be described using linear equations. This complexity derives from the extreme sensitivity of the second pendulum's momentum and position to even slight changes in the first pendulum. To know how the second pendulum will swing and therefore how the system as a whole will evolve, it would be necessary to know the starting conditions of the first pendulum *with infinite precision*. Since this is impossible, the system remains unpredictable despite its deterministic character. (pp. 8–9)

In a similar fashion, one might say that the perturbations created in journalism by narrative fiction, and vice-versa, are impossible to predict and to formalize precisely because of the impossibility of knowing the "starting conditions" of the system. Which comes first, news or narrative fiction? From a historical perspective, as Mitchell Stephens remarks, the human desire to communicate new knowledge about the environment is at least as old as narrative itself, and narrative fiction is not much newer.[13] Furthermore, narrative fiction, from the most ancient epics to the latest bestseller, always contains an element of news, either in the form of recent factual information or as a mimicry of news discourse. Conversely, news dissemination, from the earliest paleolithic grapevine to today's newspapers and networks, has always relied (without recognizing their importance) on storytelling techniques and figural language developed in the fictional realm. Indeed, it is extremely difficult to describe texts that foreground these phenomena, save in fuzzy, oxymoronic terms, such as "documentary fiction," "non-fiction novel," and "news/novel discourse" (Davis; see below), or in neologisms such as "docudrama," which I will do my best to avoid.

To attempt to enumerate the "differences" between narrative

fiction and journalism is thus obviously a trivial undertaking,
since they are first and foremost conventional and historical: at
a given point in time, certain modes of discourse have been
accepted as "journalistic" whereas others are considered "fictional." Although their aims are virtually opposite – journalism
seeks to communicate verifiable facts, narrative fiction seeks to
organize facts into aesthetically coherent wholes – at a purely
rhetorical, linguistic level, there is no way to tell one from the
other.

But if it is easy to collapse both discourses linguistically into
one another, it is unquestionable that throughout history the
"difference" between journalism and narrative fiction has been
deliberately preserved, based on the greater or lesser degree of
authority that has been assigned to either discourse. Until the
late eighteenth century, both journalism and narrative fiction
were considered lowly or marginal genres. Moreover, they were
almost interchangeable in terms of their epistemological value;
for instance, from the sixteenth to the eighteenth century in
England, Lennard Davis argues, there was a common "news/
novel discourse" shared by news ballads, newsbooks, and the
novels of Defoe and Richardson (pp. 42–70 and passim). Although novels began to be differentiated from the news/novel
discourse by the mid-eighteenth century (Davis sees Fielding as
an example of this trend, pp. 196–7), it may be argued that
much of their growing prestige in the following decades was
still owed to their connection with news and journalism's claims
of veracity. By the nineteenth century, however, the prestige of
narrative fiction, although seemingly at its zenith in the work of
the great masters of European "realist" fiction, was in fact being steadily eroded by the growing authority of science and
technology, of which journalism had become the textual
mouthpiece. Narrative fiction's claim to reveal truths of a higher order through art was severely put into question by the very
existence of journalism, which aspired to uncover truth directly, without the mediation of rhetorical artifice. Novelists and
fiction-writers in general were forced into direct confrontation
with journalism. A great many late-nineteenth-century narrators, however, still shared the values and the epistemology of
journalism and were reluctant to undertake a serious critique
of its discourse.[14]

Thus, in reply to my second question, I can now formulate the following hypothesis: During a given historical period, there *are* differences (however conventional in nature) between narrative fiction and journalism, and this makes it possible to discern traces of journalistic discourse in many literary works. These traces are numerous and varied; they range from the thematic evocation of journalism and journalists, to the outright imitation of some or all aspects of what constitutes journalistic discourse at a certain period.

The motivations for this literary mimesis of journalistic discourse are also quite varied. Since the early twentieth century in Europe, Spanish America, and the United States, the tendency has been for novelists and fiction writers to contest the authority of journalistic discourse by deconstructing it, by showing its rhetorical, artificial nature. In earlier times, however, the mimetic relation between narrative fiction and journalism seems to have been more harmonious, and, as I endeavor to show in Chapter 2 with regard to José Joaquín Fernández de Lizardi's *El Periquillo Sarniento* (1816), of an almost conspiratorial nature. From roughly the late seventeenth to the mid-nineteenth century, narrative fiction and journalism found common cause, so to speak, in a struggle against the authority of *other* discourses that claimed to hold the monopoly of truth: those of religion, the law, and the state.[15] The mutual mimesis between narrative fiction and journalism served then as a strategy against censorship, shifting information from one regulated discourse to another that was less regulated, and often proposing a subversive countervigilance to that of religion, the law, or the state (see Chapters 2 and 3).

This conflict of discourses is particularly striking in Spanish America, where journalism as a mouthpiece of modernization has frequently been a lone voice crying in a wilderness of political repression and racial and class antagonisms. Due to journalism's relative weakness in the region, the narrative fiction of Spanish America has frequently been forced to assume greater documentary and political burdens than that of Europe or North America. Furthermore, for most Spanish American writers since Fernández de Lizardi, contact with journalism as an institution has been a double-edged sword. It has provided them with a means of financial support through writing, but at the same time has imposed serious inherent constraints on their literary work. One such constraint is journalism's demotion of the "author" to mere transcriber, a *redactor de noticias* (in the eloquent Spanish phrase). Another is journalism's forcible conversion of fiction writers into something else – social crusaders, ethnologists, even politicians – distancing them from their craft and leading them to assume nonliterary roles for which they are often ill-prepared. Although the deep sense of social responsibility that permeates most Spanish American literature cannot, of course, be solely attributed to the influence of journalism, it seems clear that journalism has been one of the principal ways in which Spanish American writers have developed their social conscience. Nevertheless, Spanish American authors have also benefited from their ambiguous situation as both journalists and fiction writers. Journalism has taught them much about the nature of writing as a process and as a product, and has helped to demystify writing and the notion of "literature" itself (as we shall see in Chapter 5). Often, authors have found in the gray no-man's land between discourses the literary space that has allowed them maximum creative freedom. The relationship between journalism and literature as a whole (not just narrative fiction) in Spanish America has therefore always been particularly close and intense, despite the fiction writers' occasional efforts to distance themselves from journalism.

Lest there be any misunderstanding about my viewpoint in this book, I do not believe there is anything unique about the literature–journalism interaction in Spanish America vis-à-vis most other Western nations. I am not seeking to reaffirm in my study Spanish America's presumed cultural individuality or any reified form of national "essence." What I am saying is that in Spanish America, as in Europe and the United States, a literature–journalism interchange took place. The differences between that interchange and what took place elsewhere have been, in my view, purely contingent on Spanish America's historical circumstances. In fact, as I argue throughout this book, the literature–journalism exchange has been a means for Spanish American writers to reach for the "modernity" they see in Europe and the United States. The study of the literature–journalism link in Spanish America serves to underline the region's bond with its Western cultural heritage, even as it re-

minds us that the individual character of Spanish American
culture is not due to profound or essential structural differences, but to contingencies of historical development. In this
book I strive to be constantly aware of the role of historical
incidents and accidents in the development of Spanish American narrative, while trying to present a broad picture of that
development. I am persuaded by the arguments made in a
different, although also historically oriented, field – paleontol-
ogy – by Stephen Jay Gould:

We are creatures of endless and detailed curiosity. We are not sufficiently enlightened by abstractions devoid of flesh and bones, idio-
syncrasies and curiosities. We cannot be satisfied by concluding that a
thrust of Western history, and a dollop of geographic separation,
virtually guaranteed the eventual independence of the United States.
We want to know about the tribulations at Valley Forge, the shape of
the rude bridge that arched the flood at Concord, the reasons for
crossing out "property" and substituting "pursuit of happiness" in
Jefferson's great document. We care deeply about Darwin's encounter
with Galápagos tortoises and his studies of earthworms, orchids, and
coral reefs, even if a dozen other naturalists had carried the day for
evolution had Canning killed Castelreagh, FitzRoy sailed alone, and
Darwin become a country parson. The details do not merely embel-
lish an abstract tale moving in an inexorable way. The details are the
story itself; the underlying predictability, if discernible at all, is too
nebulous, too far in the background, and too devoid of hooks upon
actual events to count as an explanation in any satisfying sense. (pp.
29–30)

At this point it may be useful to broadly summarize, in a
narrative fashion, the history of the literature–journalism relationship in Spanish America. That history begins with the wars
of independence in the first decades of the nineteenth century.
The turmoil of independence constituted a perfect breeding
ground for journalism in Spanish America. Newspapers proliferated then, along with a variety of such other ephemeral publications as broadsides, journals, and pamphlets.[16] Although
the first newspapers had already appeared in colonial Spanish
America in the late seventeenth century, they flourished during
the wars of independence wherever the struggle against Spain
was fiercest, or, as in the case of Cuba and Puerto Rico, wherever reformist and modernizing impulses took hold among the
elite.[17] From the beginning, journalism was placed in the ser-

vice of nation-building, although the often unruly, contentious nature of the independence-era periodicals would seem to bely this: Polemic was the order of the day, and, in the multitude of voices, conservatives as well as liberals made themselves heard.[18] Nevertheless, the early Spanish American journalism, like its counterparts in the North-American and French revolutions, was imbued with the critical spirit of modernity, though it could not help but reflect the strident and uneven nature of Spanish America's particular approach to modernity as a whole.

It must be recalled that, as a rule, Spanish American journalism through the first half of the nineteenth century was divided into two broad currents: the economic or mercantile, and the political. The newspapers of former type were produced by and for the merchants and entrepreneurs. Meant to be read in the quiet of the study, or at most over the table at a coffee-house, these contained notices on the departure and arrival of ships and their type of cargo, plus essays (on political economy, medicine, "antiquities," and natural history), letters to the editor, occasional works of poetry, government proclamations (newspapers of this sort tended to be officious), and very brief bulletins on newsworthy events from around the globe. The very first daily newspapers in Spanish America, the *Diario Erudito, Económico y Comercial*, published in Lima (1790–3), and the *Diario de México* (1805–14), belong to this category (Henríquez Ureña, *Historia de la cultura en la América Hispánica*, pp. 41–2; see also Wold).

These early papers would hardly fit our current concept of a mass medium: They were printed with great difficulty, were expensive to buy, and consequently had limited circulation. Although their purpose was mainly informative, they also served as a forum for a somewhat muted ideological debate among the members of the elite during the first turbulent years of Spanish America's independence, and their style and content, with few exceptions, reflected the lofty ideals and educational propensities of the European Enlightenment. Alongside these staid publications, however, there flourished in far greater number and diversity an assortment of dailies, weeklies, pamphlets, and gazettes, devoted in their entirety to the rowdiest forms of political journalism. It was precisely journalism of this sort that

Fernández de Lizardi, the author of *El Periquillo Sarniento,* practiced in Mexico in the early nineteenth century (see Chapter 2).
The term "journalism of opinion," which is often applied to this
type of paper, hardly conveys an idea of their nature: Brazenly
partisan and often violently polemic, these publications bore
such revealing titles as *El Patriota, El Constitucional, El Indepen-
diente, El Fénix de la Libertad, El Amigo del País, El Conductor
Eléctrico,* and *El Rayo* (Henestroza and Castro, pp. 11–62). Furthermore, although accessible only to the literate elite, they
were addressed to a broader public. Their language was therefore plainer – sometimes coarse to the point of obscenity – and
more open to Spanish American idioms. Many of their articles
show the stylistic influence of oratory and drama (in their use
of the dialogue form), and were clearly meant to be read aloud
to the illiterate masses that gathered in taverns and public
squares.

Journalism was to continue to be an agent of social change
and modernization throughout the nineteenth century, despite
the increasing sanctions and restrictions imposed upon it by
postindependence authoritarian regimes that paid lip service to
liberalism or to the philosophy of Positivism, such as that of
Porfirio Díaz in Mexico. Many works of narrative fiction during
this period (literary and nonliterary) were published serially in
newspapers, from Sarmiento's *Facundo,* José Mármol's *Amalia*
(1851–5), and Manuel Payno's *Los bandidos de Río Frío* (1889–
91), to Ricardo Palma's *Tradiciones peruanas* (1872–83); others
(such as the realist and naturalist novels of the 1870s and
1890s), exhibit strong elements of journalistic discourse. Indeed, as the nineteenth century continued with the arrival of
technological improvements such as the steam-powered press
and commercial innovations such as the penny newspaper,
which increased journalism's audience enormously, the prestige
and power of journalism grew considerably – if not always vis-
à-vis the state, certainly with regard to literature, and particularly narrative fiction.

The close relationship between journalism and narrative fiction observable in Spanish America since before the period of
the wars of independence suffered profound stresses with the
arrival of the Modernists toward the turn of the century. By
then, the visibility and influence of Spanish American news-

papers, from Chile's *El Mercurio* (founded 1827) and Lima's *El Comercio* (founded 1839) to Argentina's *La Nación* (founded 1870), had reached their zenith.[19] Even as they worked in journalism, the Modernists began to conceive of themselves as professional writers and artists, and to complain bitterly of journalism's commercialization of writing and its implicit devaluation of literature as art. They struck back at the restrictions imposed upon them by journalistic discourse, evolving a highly decorative style crammed with vivid metaphors and a superabundance of literary and cultural allusions, a style that implicitly challenged journalism's utilitarian and informative demands. Despite their work in the turn-of-the-century newspapers and their avowed desire for modernization, the Modernists affirmed journalism's fundamental incompatibility with literature as an art.

This impasse began to be broken by the avant-garde writers of the early 1920s, who, in Spanish America as in Europe, produced an implicit critique of the empiricist and utilitarian nature of journalism. They achieved this by adopting and adapting into their own works numerous aspects of journalistic discourse, even at the visual level (for example, the use of collagelike techniques and the insistence on the typographic aspect of texts). By showing that journalistic discourse could be successfully imitated by literature, the avant-gardists and their successors made clear the common rhetorical and linguistic basis of both forms of discourse, and undermined journalism's implicit claim to superiority over literature because of its supposedly greater proximity to "reality" or "truth." This paved the way for the more egalitarian relationship between both modes of discourse evident in Spanish American literature today. Lately, contemporary Spanish American writers have become less preoccupied with the truth-claims of journalism and more concerned with the growing power and influence of the electronic mass media, which seem to threaten the relevance and importance of both literature and print journalism.[20] Also, as I argue in Chapter 6, Spanish American writers since the novelistic "boom" of the sixties have tended to inscribe journalism into their works as a metaphor for ethics and as a means to develop what I call (modifying a title by J. Hillis Miller, *The Ethics of Reading*) an "ethics of writing."

Modernity, journalism, and narrative fiction have interacted in Spanish American history in a distinctive way. Journalism has served to "textualize" modernity and to import its ideology into the Spanish American intellectual milieu. For its part, since its early years Spanish American narrative fiction has tended to work in consonance with the modernizing impulse fostered by journalism, often making strategic use of elements of journalistic discourse to serve an agenda of social or political change. As modernity seemed to triumph in Spanish America at the turn of the nineteenth century, though, narrative fiction and poetry began to be conceived of in more autonomous terms, and a conflict ensued between the institution of journalism (on which writers came to depend for their professional existence) and the idea of literature as an end in itself. This conflict was finally resolved in the twentieth century by a critique of journalistic discourse that pointed out its rhetorical commonality with fictional discourse. Simultaneously, the turn-of-the century struggle with journalism served to modernize (and eventually corrode) the idea of literature generated by nineteenth-century writers. Literature and journalism began to be seen as diverse assortments of texts linked to each other in a nonhierarchical way. However, even as narrative fiction and journalism have recovered their common ground, new modes of communication, such as the electronic mass media, have challenged the authority of writing and textuality, and have led fiction writers to seek out in journalism clues with which to explore the nature of fundamental concepts such as "authority" and "communication."

The highly schematic account I have just given of the interactions between modernity, journalism, and literature in Spanish America is essentially the story this book attempts to tell in greater detail. The way it is told, however, will continue to be schematic at a historical level: This book is not a history, neither of Spanish American journalism nor of Spanish American literature. Its focus is nonetheless decidedly literary; in other words, this is primarily a book of literary criticism and theory, not a work of journalistic theory (although some of its observations about journalism might have theoretical applications). I have chosen to comment on only a few texts, most of which are considered important in the conventional canon of Spanish

American literature: *El Periquillo Sarniento* (Chapter 2), *Facundo* (Chapter 3), *Tradiciones peruanas* (Chapter 4) and texts by Martí (Chapter 5) and Borges and García Márquez (Chapter 6). Although all of these are narratives (even the Modernist chronicles), some are of dubious fictional status, and the "literary" status of others is still debatable. On the whole, the novelty of my approach lies not so much in proposing canonic revisions as in promoting reinterpretations of already canonized works. Nevertheless, as the book's focus moves closer to the present time, my choice of texts to analyze becomes less canonical (in my discussion of documentary fiction I examine works by Elena Poniatowska, who has only recently achieved canonic recognition). The chapters are organized in an episodic manner, following a historical sequence: They are to be seen as "snapshots," or as case studies, of certain key moments in the history of the literature–journalism relationship in Spanish America. Although my approach is highly historicist, I share Paul de Man's reservations toward literary history (positivistic or otherwise) as well as the intrinsic interpretation of literature. Befitting such a turbulent and uncertain situation, my discourse therefore shifts deliberately and strategically back and forth from literary and cultural history to deconstructive readings – hopefully without unduly privileging either one – in order to illuminate important aspects of Spanish American narrative fiction. If it also happens to shed light on more general questions of Spanish American culture and the role of journalism within it, this will be only an accidental result of a deliberately partial and modest inquiry into the origins and development of Spanish American narrative fiction.

2

Journalism and (dis)simulation in
El Periquillo Sarniento

> *The butterfly turned into a leaf, the man turned into a woman, but also anamorphosis and trompe-l'oeil, do not copy, are not justified and defined on the basis of true proportions, but instead produce, using the observer's position, bringing him into the imposture, the model's verisimilitude: they incorporate, as in a predatory act, its appearance, they simulate it.*
>
> Severo Sarduy, *La simulación* (1982)

> *His name was Loulou. His body was green, the tips of his wings were pink, his poll blue, and his breast golden.*
>
> Gustave Flaubert, "A Simple Heart" (1877)

The first work of narrative prose in Spanish America to openly proclaim itself a work of fiction and to associate itself with the novel is *El Periquillo Sarniento* (1816), by the Mexican pamphleteer José Joaquín Fernández de Lizardi. Elevated to a classic by the Spanish American critical tradition, *El Periquillo*, like many other classics, is more talked-about than read. Although a substantial body of criticism has already accreted around it, much of that consists of repetitions of prior judgments by earlier analysts of Lizardi's text or of readings that are more attentive to the sociocultural and lexicographic information contained in the text than to its intrinsic formal and rhetorical attributes.[1] Valued mostly for its depiction of the manners and mores of early nineteenth-century Mexico, essentially as a precursor of *costumbrismo*, scant attention has been paid to its figural elements.[2] Readers of Lizardi's work have generally busied themselves with what the text signifies at an extratextual level – its literary and cultural allusions, the information it provides about society, politics, and language in independence-era Mexico, or its thematic links with Lizardi's pamphleteering – and

21

have not paid sufficient attention to the system of tropes by means of which Lizardi gives his text the illusion of coherence and narrative flow. Although my ultimate aim is to explore the relationship between *El Periquillo* and Lizardi's journalism, I believe this should not be done without at least attempting to read the text on its own terms – that is, in terms of its rhetoric and its strategies of representation.

An overly hasty linkage of Lizardi's discourse in *El Periquillo* to that of Enlightenment texts has led to a largely un-problematical view of its use of language and representational strategies. To twentieth-century readers, Lizardi's narrative voice, like that of such Enlightenment authors as Voltaire, Rousseau, and Diderot, sounds modern and transparent; it speaks with a commonsensical, down-to-earth style that seeks a middle ground between the aristocratic and plebleian usages, and emphasizes maximum communicative effectiveness. *El Periquillo's* discourse deliberately eschews many of the elements associated with Baroque style, particularly the use of Latin quotations, but also the convoluted Latinate syntax of *culteranismo* and the ponderous metaphorical imagery of *conceptismo*. Nevertheless, *El Periquillo* still clearly retains many Baroque elements in its discourse, beginning with its allusions to the Spanish picaresque tradition and to topics such as *desengaño*. It is furthermore naive to assume that because Enlightenment rhetorical norms emphasized linguistic clarity and effectiveness, such a use of language was devoid of tropes and metaphors of its own. As I attempt to show, *El Periquillo's* discourse is built around the tropes of simulation and dissimulation (both meanings of Lizardi's term *fingir*, which I will condense as "[dis]simulation"); these tropes are in turn connected with the image of the parrot that is used to allude both to the text and to its protagonist, and they are also linked to the theme of hypocrisy that runs through the text. The image of the parrot recurs in Lizardi's journalistic work, and is highly suggestive in terms of Lizardi's implicit theory of writing. The recurrent images of simulation, camouflage, and mimeticism in *El Periquillo* serve to elucidate how Lizardi seems to have viewed the relationship between his pamphleteering and his novelistic endeavors.

Although it was published episodically in pamphlets, *El Periquillo Sarniento* has a generally coherent and well-thought-out plot line, which its moralistic digressions (as the narrator insists time and time again) do not manage to lead astray. Unlike the *roman-feuilletons* of later decades (such as Eugène Sue's *Les Mystères de Paris*, 1842–3), the writing of *El Periquillo* appears to have been little affected by any feedback from its readers, save in one significant instance, that of the state censor, who intervened to block the publication of the text's Volume 4 due to its open polemic against slavery.[3] External evidence of the premeditated nature of *El Periquillo* may be seen in the fact that Lizardi published a prospectus of his text before beginning publication of the complete work (Spell, *Bridging the Gap*, p. 145). In the text itself, the reappearance at key moments of various characters, such as Januario, Aguilita, Don Antonio, and *el trapiento* (the Raggedy Man), signals Lizardi's intention of giving his work a coherent structure, even if it meant involving his protagonist in a series of improbably coincidental and repetitious encounters. Indeed, redundancy is a salient quality of this text, which often repeats the same message using different characters and scenes; for example, the moral lesson that "clothes do not make the man" is repeated countless times in Periquillo's experience, sometimes discursively, as in Don Antonio's advice upon leaving prison (p. 193; see below), sometimes by example, as in the case of the Raggedy Man (in Chapter 8 of the second part).

The most effective way to examine the related tropes of simulation and dissimulation in *El Periquillo* is to follow the text's plotline, since to a large extent the work is concerned with its protagonist's education in the "dos and don'ts" of *fingir*. In general, the work recounts the life of Pedro Sarmiento, a dissipated youth from the impoverished creole middle class of late-Colonial Mexico. Like the picaresque narratives it resembles, the text is presented as a first-person written account, in this case blatantly confessional, penned on his deathbed by the reformed narrator as a cautionary tale for his children. Because of this, *El Periquillo* offers what might be called a "bifocal" perspective: The narrator seeks to convey the thoughts and feelings he had in the past, but he also often comments critically on them from his present "reformed" condition. The story begins with his birth in 1771 or 1773 (the uncertainty in dates is the narrator's, p. 12) in Mexico City, the only son of creole middle

class parents, and goes on to tell of his upbringing and education. From the beginning, we see the young Pedro Sarmiento
caught in a tug-of-war between virtue and vice: Instead of being nursed by his mother, he is given a nursemaid (a practice
considered pernicious by the narrator, pp. 13–14); his father,
although a constant source of sensible advice, is never strong
enough to counteract the mother's vain and frivolous influence
on her son's character (pp. 14–16).

In Pedro's early schooling, we find similar ambiguities and
tensions. His first schoolteacher is a bumbling incompetent who
eventually resigns his post (p. 23), and, after a brief interlude
with a harsh and disciplinarian instructor (p. 24), young Pedro
is placed with an exemplary schoolteacher (pp. 25–7) who
seems to have been lifted from the pages of Rousseau's *Emile*
(1762).[4] It is under his first schoolteacher that his classmates
give Pedro the nickname he will carry for the rest of his life and
which will become emblematic in more ways than one. As the
narrator explains, "I went to school in a green jacket and yellow
trousers. These colors, and the fact that my teacher sometimes
referred to me affectionately as *Pedrillo,* inspired my friends to
give me my nickname, which was *Periquillo;* but I needed an
adjective or surname to distinguish myself from another *Perico*
who was among us, and did not take long in getting it. I caught
an itching illness [*sarna*] and no sooner did my classmates notice
it than, remembering my true surname, they forced upon me
the resounding title of *Sarniento*" (p. 21).

"Periquillo Sarniento" (which translates as "Little Itching Parrot"),[5] like the names and nicknames of other characters in the
text (such as Januario, or Doctor Purgante), is fraught with
symbolism and verges on allegory. The first half – "Periquillo"
– prefigures Pedro's mimetic propensities, not only his attempts to make a living through deception and appearances,
but also his habit of falling under the spell of any reasonably
persuasive person, whether good or bad. It also anticipates his
verbal proclivities, his talkativeness, and his penchant for oratorical digressions late in life. The second half – "Sarniento" –
alludes not only to the character's poverty throughout most of
his life, but also, since whoever itches must scratch himself, it
implicitly prefigures Pedro's restless, ambulatory life.

Despite his father's wishes that he study a trade (such as

cobbling or tailoring), Periquillo is enrolled in philosophy in the Colegio de San Ildefonso. He receives his baccalaureate after two and a half years of indifferent studies, in which he merely learns impressive-sounding Latin phrases and scientific terminology (pp. 38–40). Full of himself, he is sent by his parents, as a graduation present, to spend some days at the rural estate of a friend of his father's. It is there, in the company of his schoolmate Januario that he receives his first major lesson in dissimulation. In fact, it is the aptly named Januario – his name alludes to the double-faced Roman deity of crossroads, as well as to his double-crossing nature – who causes the event, when he incites Periquillo to show off his spurious knowledge about comets before the dinner guests, like a Cantiflas *avant la lettre* or like a parrot (pp. 45–6). A vicar among the guests then contradicts and corrects him with a long and learned disquisition about the subject, leaving Periquillo utterly embarrassed (pp. 47–8). But Periquillo's mimeticism saves him from total disgrace when he decides to approach the priest, confess his ignorance, and ask him where he can read more about comets; to all this the priest responds favorably, and Periquillo is instantly *prendado de su bello carácter* ("charmed by his beautiful moral disposition," p. 49). This priest is but one in a series of "positive" characters whose goodness Periquillo will seek to emulate as long as he remains in their proximity. Once they are gone, however, he is left adrift until he finds another he can imitate; one who is usually, by way of contrast, of a dishonest disposition.

Still seeking to avoid becoming a tradesman or artisan, Periquillo persuades his father to let him study for the priesthood, since he is convinced that this will be the easiest way for him to earn a living. While he nominally studies theology, he is in fact becoming a disciple of Januario, who instructs him in gambling, whoring, and party-going (pp. 75–7). When his father discovers Periquillo's duplicity, he once again enjoins him to enter a trade. This time, Periquillo appeals to another dissolute friend, theology student Martín Pelayo, who advises him to become a friar and through family connections gets him admitted into the monastery of San Diego (pp. 80–3). Periquillo's mother, who is always portrayed as naive, vain, and convinced that she is of noble lineage, believes therefore that her son should aspire only to those professions considered honorable for *hidalgos* and

manages to persuade her husband to allow Periquillo's entry
into the religious order (pp. 84–5). Periquillo has lasted barely
six months in the convent, and he is already "thinking about
which illness it would be convenient to have, or simulate having" (p. 92) in order to be discharged from the convent, when
he receives news of his father's death (p. 92). Now that his
father is dead, Periquillo leaves the order, returns home to live
with his mother, and, after six months of mourning and good
behavior, happily proceeds to spend all his inheritance on gambling, women, and parties, leaving his mother in abject poverty.
Soon after, his mother dies having realized her son is a dissolute
idler, and Periquillo once again appeals to his friend Januario.
The latter convinces Periquillo to join him in making a living as
a *cócora,* a parasitic cardsharp who hangs around players who
have money, barges into card games claiming to have made a
bet, and, in the confusion over whose money is on the table,
runs off with the money (pp. 127–8).

His misadventures as a gambler leave Periquillo wounded in a
hospital (pp. 145–54), from which he is discharged after three
days. Januario then tries to persuade him to become a burglar,
an activity at which Periquillo draws the line (pp. 152–5), although he is not strong enough to resist following Januario on
his excursion. Although innocent, he is accused of complicity
with Januario because he is wearing Januario's *zarape* and a
rosary the latter had stolen, and he is thrown into jail (pp. 156–
7). There he meets two contrasting characters who, once again,
influence him in opposite ways: the kindly Don Antonio, an
honest provincial merchant from Orizaba who has been un-
justly imprisoned by the machinations of an evil marquis, and
the sinister Aguilita or Aguilucho (both names are used to refer
to him), a habitual thief.

Periquillo's imprisonment offers him further lessons in the
values of appearance and dissimulation. To begin, it is his
youthful and innocent demeanor that motivates Don Antonio's
sympathy and leads the latter into offering to share his cell and
his meals with Periquillo (p. 159); similarly, Periquillo judges
Don Antonio to be a different sort of prisoner because he was
blanco y no de mala presencia ("white and not bad in appearance,"
p. 158). We see here Periquillo's growing awareness of the codes
used to distinguish one caste from another in Colonial Mexican

society: He and Don Antonio recognize each other as members of the white creole group among a crowd of mostly mestizo and mulatto prisoners; their similar appearance leads each to regard the other as, at least potentially, an *"hombre de bien"* ("an honest man," p. 159).

The lengthy tale of woe Don Antonio recounts to Periquillo in their cell is one of the clearest manifestations of this text's links with the tradition of eighteenth-century sentimental narrative (of which more is said later in this chapter), but it is also a lesson about how the codes used to identify *hombres de bien* can be misread and used to deceive. The apparently honorable Marquis of T. used an elaborate economic ruse to keep Don Antonio's beautiful young wife by his side in Mexico City while the merchant was sent on a lengthy business trip on the marquis' behalf. When the wife virtuously resisted the marquis' blandishments, the latter decided to avenge himself by accusing Don Antonio of carrying contraband tobacco, and thus the merchant ended up in jail with Periquillo. Throughout his story, Don Antonio stresses the marquis' duplicity and his own need to maintain his composure before the marquis, even after knowing the latter had tried to seduce his wife, so as not to provoke even further his powerful adversary ("I was obliged to dissimulate and condescend [*me fue forzoso disimular y condescender*]," p. 181). Don Antonio's story ends happily, however, since shortly after Periquillo meets him, he is freed from jail: Repenting on his deathbed, the marquis had written a letter exculpating the merchant and asking for his forgiveness (p. 183). Before leaving, Don Antonio enjoins Periquillo to avoid friendship with some of the other prisoners,

not because they are poor or dark, since these are accidents by which men should not be despised nor their company shunned, particularly if such color and such rags cover, as may happen, a virtuous nature, but because this is not what is usually done; a common birth and personal extravagance are usually the surest signals of their utter lack of education and good upbringing. (p. 193)

However, this lesson in social and moral semiotics remains ambiguous for Periquillo as well as for the reader: If neither visual cues (such as skin color or style of clothing) nor behavioral cues (the courtesy and good manners of the marquis, for example) are reliable indicators of "a virtuous nature," how can Periquillo be sure his friends are *hombres de bien?* Not surprisingly, as soon as Don Antonio leaves, Periquillo is drawn toward the mulatto Aguilita, whose avian nickname ("Little Eagle") already suggests a bond with Periquillo.

These two jailbirds are not wholly birds of a feather, of course: Aguilita is a sharp-eyed, quick-clawed predator (p. 195), whereas Periquillo is a scavenger and a mimic. Paradoxically, it is Periquillo's parrotlike imitativeness, his desire to blend in, which makes him easy prey to Aguilita's robberies inside the jail (pp. 201–2). Periquillo is not, after all, a chameleon whose mimeticism protects him from predators (or allows him to become one); his imitative behavior, like a parrot's, is mostly spontaneous and unmotivated, lacking in true understanding. Even when he realizes what has happened, he feigns ignorance:

I began to think that scoundrel [Aguilita] had been the principal agent of my robbery, as he indeed turned out to be, but I did not let on that I knew, because I figured that I would make myself hateful to those people. . . . With this dissimulation we got by, with my receiving drinks of liquor in exchange for the food I gave to that sparrow hawk. (pp. 201–2)

Periquillo's exit from the jail begins a whole series of new transformations, new disguises. In a typically picaresque movement, he goes from one master to another; nevertheless, far from remaining a mere servant, he learns to simulate the behavior and abilities of his masters to the point of taking their place, albeit temporarily. Thus he becomes, in quick succession: secretary to the notary lawyer Chanfaina, from whom he learns tricks of legalistic rhetoric ("the art of kabbalistic penmanship [*el arte de la cábala con la pluma*]," p. 213); apprentice to a barber (he never learns to shave others or do tooth extractions properly, pp. 224–8); assistant to the druggist Don José, whom he impresses with his rudimentary knowledge of Latin and by his hypocritical behavior (p. 231), until he accidentally poisons a customer (p. 233); and, lastly, assistant to the Molieresque Doctor Purgante, from whom he learns to use Latinate and Baroque medical jargon so convincingly that after stealing some of his books, diplomas, and clothing, he is able to leave his master and pass himself off as a doctor in the small town of Tula (pp. 235–47). By then, Periquillo's education in lying and deceit has reached its peak, and his own personality has become profoundly ambiguous and mysterious even to himself, as the already-"reformed" narrator explains:

Such was sometimes my cunning and, sometimes, my ignorance. I myself am now incapable of defining my character during those times, and I believe nobody else would have been able to understand it, because on some occasions I said what I felt, but on others I acted against my very words. At times I became a hypocrite, at others I spoke my conscience; but the worst was that when I feigned virtue I did it knowingly, and when I became enamoured of it, I innerly resolved a thousand times to mend my ways, but never had the will to fulfill my resolutions. (p. 223)

As I have already remarked, Periquillo's mimeticism expresses itself not only verbally and behaviorally, but in terms of dress as well. Each of his mutations is expressed by a different (dis)guise; the many rises and falls in his fortunes are marked by periodic changes of clothing, like an actor returning to his dressing room. Whenever he is down and out, his clothing immediately reflects this, but even then there are gradations: sometimes his rags are those of a white beggar or vagrant; at other times he sinks lower in the social pyramid and ends up dressed like an Indian (p. 397). But clothing is more than a mere reflection of his social status; Periquillo understands perfectly that in his society clothes *do* make the man, and he consciously uses them on many occasions to improve his social condition by simulating a status he does not possess (such as when he passes himself off as a doctor, wearing the robes and wigs he has stolen from Doctor Purgante). However, it is important to stress, as the narrator frequently does, the inadequacy of Periquillo's mimeticism: Despite his best efforts, in the end he is unmasked by circumstances or by his own clumsiness, and people always see through his (dis)guise. Further episodes reiterate not only Periquillo's tactics of (dis)simulation, but his increasing view of life as a play of appearances, which culminates in his very Baroque *desengaño* in Chapter 10 of the third part. Before that, he has already experienced the irony of his own mimetic success, when, in a complex scene, Periquillo's erstwhile friend Anselmo feigns not to recognize him when he sees him turned into a beggar, and tells him: "Don Pedro Sarmiento, whom you resemble somewhat, is indeed my friend; but he is a well-bred man, an honest man, and a man of means; not a thieving, half-naked vagrant" (p. 398).

In the context of Periquillo's gradual movement toward disillusionment, the story's longest and most blatant digression comes into sharper focus: This is, of course, Periquillo's travel to Manila in the service of the Colonel (pp. 323–55), and his shipwreck on an unnamed island in the South China Sea (pp. 356–79). His sojourn in Manila with the virtuous Colonel is for Periquillo an education in the values of moderate self-love and philanthropy. The episode of the egotist (pp. 332–40) and the dialogue between an Englishman and a wealthy black merchant on the subject of slavery (pp. 343–50) are object lessons on the evils of inordinate self-love and the need to love one's fellows. Moreover, if for Periquillo life in Mexico was like being on a crowded stage in a play in which all the leading roles have been distributed, the Orient is conversely a nearly empty stage, an almost-blank space in which Periquillo, relatively unconstrained by the hierarchical pressures of Colonial Mexican society, often finds himself alone, a figurative castaway – as he later indeed literally becomes.[6] Thus in Manila he appears more self-possessed, and finds it easier to be *un hombre de bien a toda prueba* (p. 343), particularly with the strong example of the Colonel nearby. After the Colonel dies, however, leaving Periquillo a substantial inheritance, Periquillo begins to lose his newfound self-possession, and he fantasizes, on the ship that takes him back to the New World, that he will one day become Viceroy of Mexico (pp. 356–7). This fantasy is interrupted by a storm that shipwrecks him on an unnamed island governed by wise "Chinese" (*chinos*), who insist that he must make himself useful to his new society by learning a trade (pp. 359–64). Periquillo then proceeds to take full advantage of his new and still-undefined social status in the island, of the almost-empty stage (there are just two other Westerners in the island). He tells his hosts that in his land he is a count, which – he then explains – means that he is wealthy and cannot engage in manual labor. His dissembling is almost uncovered by one of the two foreigners, a Spanish nobleman, who asks Periquillo for his title, since he knows personally all the titled nobility in Mexico. Periquillo barely carries off his charade by pretending to be recently titled (p. 367).

Periquillo returns to Mexico in the company of his erstwhile Chinese host, who soon discovers that his Mexican friend is no member of the nobility (p. 384). Despite this, the Chinese generously decides Periquillo's has been an innocent lie, since he judges him to be an *hombre de bien* (p. 384), and accepts him as his servant and *cicerone* in Mexico City. This does not last long, of course, and Periquillo quickly finds himself back in utter destitution.

Periquillo's final conversion can be seen as the result of both his gradual process of disillusionment – his growing awareness of (dis)simulation as a norm in his society – and the death of the two main representatives of vice and hypocrisy in the text, Januario and Aguilita. The latter is killed, along with several members of his band of outlaws who terrorized the approaches to Río Frío, in an encounter with armed merchants. He had found the beggared Periquillo weeks earlier on the road and forced him to join his band, despite Periquillo's verbose pleas that he was too much of a coward to become a bandit (pp. 405–6). Januario's hanged corpse is found by Periquillo shortly after the shootout in which Aguilita is killed; Periquillo's hypocritical childhood friend had also become a bandit (pp. 416–17).

With the two most powerful negative influences on Periquillo's life permanently out of the picture, the perennial tug-of-war in the text between virtue and vice resolves itself in favor of virtue. Nevertheless, although it seemingly follows from the logic of the text, Periquillo's conversion still appears arbitrary: such a conversion could have come at many other earlier moments when Periquillo was almost equally destitute and battered, yet it did not. Although the narrator insists that Periquillo had in him the makings of an *hombre de bien*, there is no explanation, within the character's own logic, of his sudden abandonment of dissimulation. He is, after all, the Little Itching Parrot, and has spent his life in one continuous effort at simulation; why should we believe he has stopped doing so, that his conversion is authentic, and not another dissimulation in a chain that could go on until his death?

One answer might lie in this narrative's partly allegorical nature. As I have already remarked, Periquillo as a character possesses strong allegorical elements, and so do many of the other characters in the text, from Januario to Doctor Purgante and Aguilita. Despite its appeals to reasonableness and to Enlightenment ideology, *El Periquillo Sarniento* makes abundant use of rhetorical devices, such as allegory, which were perennially associated with religious dogma but had maintained their importance in the popular culture of the Hispanic world. Periquillo's final conversion may be seen as an instance of allegory's dogmatic nature: The story has been told, the lesson has been taught with numerous (perhaps too many) examples, and now the moral must be expressed. I would, however, stress the weakness of the narrator's attempt at closure compared to the force of Periquillo's mimetic impulse. There seems to be no way out of the logic of (dis)simulation; once he has become a hypocrite and a liar, there is no means of shoring up the eroded foundations of the narrator's reliability.

One common trait of allegorical characters, as Angus Fletcher reminds us, is that they always appear to be driven by forces outside of themselves, propelled by the ideas they ultimately embody: thus, Januario can be seen as an archetypal Betrayer; Doctor Purgante as the prototype of the Charlatan.[7] Periquillo himself is a more complex figure: He is not quite Everyman, nor is he merely an allegory of Hypocrisy; he is more likely, I would argue, an allegory of the Journalist or perhaps in more general terms, of Writing itself (at least, as Lizardi understood this concept). Indeed, one possible way of reconciling the narrator's unreliability with his insistence that he has truly converted into a God-fearing *hombre de bien* is to posit that Periquillo has managed to displace his penchant for dissimulation, verbosity, and mimicry into another area of life: writing. The text strongly suggests this displacement on two occasions when Periquillo composes poems. Both instances occur toward the end of the narrative, and both are associated with death: first, when Periquillo, after being dismissed by the Chinese, ends up dressed as an Indian and attends a poor man's funeral, he composes some *décimas* (p. 401); and second, when he finds the body of Januario, he inscribes a sonnet with a knife on a nearby tree (p. 417). Both texts are expressions of *desengaño*, but they also point to Periquillo's nascent writerly vocation, which ultimately results in the writing of the text of *El Periquillo Sarniento*.

In writing his deathbed memoirs, Periquillo focuses his mimetic, simulatory skills on written language, though this time with a less self-centered motivation. His aim, as he states in his prologue (p. 5) and repeats throughout the text, is to educate his children in the moral pitfalls of life by means of the fictional representation of vice and its consequences. Like the Archpriest of Hita, in the medieval *Book of Good Love*, Periquillo dissimulates – lies – in his text in order to lead his readers, allegorically, toward a higher truth. Nevertheless, he seems to be aware that the displacement of dissimulation toward writing does not close off such a process, nor is dissimulation made less problematic when it is reduced to the realm of writing and to "educational" purposes. That is why in the end he must simply command his readers – among whom are his sons – not to dissimulate, and particularly not to imitate him:

God forbid that after the end of my days you should abandon yourselves to vice, and take only your father's bad example, perhaps with the foolish hope of making amends, as he did, in the middle of your life, nor that you should say in the secrecy of your heart: "Let us follow our father in his mistakes, for we will later follow him in his change of behavior, since perhaps such iniquitous hopes will not be realized." (p. 452)

In *Dissemination*, Jacques Derrida has called attention to the Platonic metaphor of Writing (in *Phaedrus*) as a wandering orphan of dubious ancestry who therefore occupies a marginal, even subversive, position in society (pp. 77–84). The orphaned and delinquent Periquillo's final conversion into a writer, as well as his links with unmotivated language suggested by his nickname, "Little Parrot," indicate that Lizardi is working within a problematic similar to Plato's.

To elucidate this, we must reflect further on the image of the parrot which in so many ways presides over this text. This image is an important key to deciphering the allegory of *El Periquillo Sarniento*. The parrot seems to us today (particularly after its use in Flaubert's "A Simple Heart") such an obvious symbol of purposeless mimicry that Lizardi's appropriation of it appears altogether natural; nevertheless, as is clear from the very text of *El Periquillo*, the notion of "originality" was still quite foreign to Lizardi, and he probably derived this image from the emblematic and fabulistic tradition.[8] In Tomás de Iriarte's *Fábulas literarias* (1780), a work well-known to Lizardi, the parrot, although seen as an emblem of vacuity, foolishness, mimicry, and linguistic alienation, is also consistently associated with the figure of the writer ("Fábulas" V, XXIV, XXXVIII, LXXI). This association of the parrot with writing is logically consistent with the Platonic tradition, which views writing as a kind of alienated language, a voice without a consciousness to give it coherence and truthfulness. What we have in the character of Periquillo Sarniento is a sort of reduplication, an intensification – more in the spirit of the Baroque than of the Enlightenment – of this Platonic topic: An orphan, a "parrot," and a writer, Periquillo is a triple emblem of writing.

Lizardi also penned numerous fables, and the parrot is prominent in two of them: "El mono y el perico," in *Alacena de frioleras*, No. 11 (1815; *Obras, IV*, pp. 67–72), and "El loro en la tertulia," in *Fábulas* (1817; *Obras, I*, pp. 365–7). Unlike Iriarte, Lizardi does not explicitly link the parrot with writers, but there is a similar ambiguity in both authors' use of this figure: Although the parrot frequently appears foolish or insane, it can occasionally, like fools or madmen, speak the truth (Lizardi, "El mono y el perico;" Iriarte, "Fábulas" V, XXXVIII). This ambiguity is clearly exploited by Lizardi in *El Periquillo*. Periquillo may be a "parrot," but he can still speak wisely at times; indeed, in the repressive society in which he lives, only a talkative, irresponsible dissembler like he is can get away with making statements critical of society and authority.

The close parallels between Periquillo and Lizardi are laid out quite explicitly near the end of the text. There, we learn that the fictional editor of Periquillo's manuscript is "*El Pensador Mexicano*" (Lizardi's pseudonym). Of this character, Periquillo says (with a wink to his readers) that "we have loved each other so much that I can safely say that I am one with *el Pensador* and he with me" (p. 454). It becomes clear that most of Periquillo's attributes are shared by the Mexican pamphleteer who is the real-world author of his narrative, and that *El Periquillo Sarniento* can also be read as an allegorical discourse about writers and journalists in Colonial Mexico. The clincher to this

Periquillo–Lizardi connection may be the fact that Lizardi gave
two of his late pamphlets titles that seem to allude to his novel:
La Victoria del Perico (The Parrot's Victory, 1823) and *El Her-
mano del Perico que Cantaba la Victoria* (The Brother of the Parrot
who Sang Victory, 1823). In the latter, as Jacobo Checinsky
describes it, "the author imagines . . . an enlightened parrot –
the reincarnation of Pythagoras, no less – with whom he holds
a series of dialogues in which the advantages of liberal federal-
ism *versus* conservative centralism are discussed" (*Obras*, III,
18).

What then is the allegorical message encoded in Periquillo, in
his parrotlike imitativeness, and his misadventures? What does
the text have to tell us about writing, journalistic writing in
particular? *El Periquillo Sarniento*, as I have noted before, is
redundant; that is, it didactically repeats its lesson many times
in different ways and with different degrees of explicitness. In
my view, one of the most explicit and condensed passages in
this regard occurs in Chapter 4 of the third part, when Periquillo tries to pass himself off as a count on the island of the
"Chinese." Reflecting on how well he was treated by everyone
because they thought he was someone important, Periquillo
muses on the pros and cons of *fingir*:

The world most often values men not for their real titles but for those
they claim to have.
    Despite this, I do not say that to feign [*fingir*] is good, however
useful it may be to those who feign. Cheats and go-betweens also find
their tricks and dissimulations useful, yet they are not lawful. What I
want you to get from this story is the realization of how vulnerable we
are to being tricked by any sly picaroon who makes us believe ourselves giants of nobility, talent, and wealth. We fall for his persuasion –
what they call *labia* [winning eloquence] – he bilks us if he can, trick-
ing us always, and we realize we have been had only when it is too late
to stop it. In any case, my sons, you must study man, observe him,
penetrate into his soul; watch the way he operates, disregarding the
exteriors of dress, titles, and income, and as soon as you find someone
who always speaks truthfully and doesn't stick to his own advantage
like iron to a magnet, trust him, and say: this is an honest man [*hombre
de bien*], this one will not trick me, nor will I receive harm from him.
But in order to find this man, you will have to ask Diogenes for his
lantern. (p. 369)

In this meditation on *fingir,* which is also a meditation on
reading and interpreting, the narrator again shows his aware-

ness of the profoundly deceptive nature of language (and indeed, of any communicative code), which can be harnessed to any purpose, good or bad. All language is liable to become alienated, corrupted, and perverted, like that of the parrot, torn from its origins or moorings in a rational consciousness – in other words, to become like writing. We must learn to read correctly, Lizardi states, in order not to be tricked by a hostile and devious world. Alarmingly, however, Lizardi also states that we will probably always be tricked anyway. The essence of his lesson is a feeling of vulnerability, an awareness of the perils facing the reader in a world that abounds in people with *labia*, with eloquence, who will repeat and distort words in order to take advantage of others. Like Rousseau, Lizardi seems to regard writing as a "dangerous supplement,"[9] a double-faced activity that can help as well as hinder, improve as well as corrupt, and which must be kept in check by the application of an inner moral sense. Here Lizardi's links with the tradition of eighteenth-century sentimental narrative come to the fore: Lizardi professes to believe that humanity is ultimately innately good, and that, given the opportunity, it will spontaneously tend toward order, reason, and benevolence.[10]

El Periquillo Sarniento is itself an act of dissimulation, a textual camouflage. And, like any good camouflage, as Sarduy reminds us in the epigraph to this chapter, it entails a modicum of self-revelation – a certain brazenness, such as that of the butterfly that hides itself by *displaying itself* as a leaf. Important among the autobiographical elements from Lizardi's life in *El Periquillo* are his reflections on his own career as a journalist, and his attempt at self-justification. Periquillo's constant imitativeness, his desperate desire to be liked and accepted by all and to achieve success through simulation, exactly parallels Lizardi's own dependence on the public's fickleness and the authorities' tolerance toward his making a living as a pamphleteer. And although Lizardi, unlike Periquillo, does not seem to have sought wealth and status, he clearly understood the attraction of the peculiar form of power inherent in journalism, one which emanates from the figural use of language, from simulation.[11] In *El Periquillo*, Lizardi presents an allegory of his own career as a pamphleteer in early-nineteenth-century Mexico: It is the journalist as *pícaro*, living by his wits, relying on many masters (his readers),[12] using the figural, dissimulating powers of language to attract some readers and to protect himself from others. The facts of Lizardi's biography – his hand-to-mouth existence, his frequent troubles with the authorities, his imprisonments – tend to support such a view. The main difference between Periquillo and his author may lie in Lizardi's passionate engagement with politics, which Periquillo does not show but which seems to have fueled Lizardi's vocation as a journalist. But even in political matters Lizardi was forced to dissemble, since his reformist views frequently put him at odds with the government and the church.

Lizardi's greatest act of dissimulation, I would argue, is *El Periquillo Sarniento* itself: a text that is fundamentally a pamphlet passing itself off as a work of narrative fiction, as an "*obra romancesca*" (Lizardi's own phrase, p. 7). Save for its plot, there is little to distinguish *El Periquillo* from the hundreds of other pamphlets Lizardi had already published and would continue to publish after the restrictions on his journalism were lifted in 1820. Any reader of Lizardi's newspapers, from *El Pensador Mexicano* (1812–13), *Alacena de frioleras* (1815–16), and *El Caxoncito de la Alacena* (1815–16), to *El Conductor Eléctrico* (1820), among others, cannot fail to notice the nearly absolute similarity between the writing of *El Periquillo* and the dialogues, fables, narratives, and polemics about current events that comprise the bulk of the material in these publications. Dialogues such as that between a young girl and "Tata Pablo" in Issue 13, Volume 1, of *El Pensador Mexicano* (*Obras, III*, pp. 114–18), or between "El Tío Toribio" and his nephew Juanillo in Issue 6, Volume 2 (*Obras, III*, pp. 181–9), could easily have been included in the text of *El Periquillo*, so could the comments on the "abuses of fashion" in Volume 2 of the Supplements to *El Pensador* (*Obras, III*, pp. 317–20) and the satirical poems and fables scattered throughout most of the issues of Lizardi's first important newspaper, to mention just a few examples. And, needless to say, Lizardi's journalistic style was not particularly unique; other newspapers in Mexico and the rest of the Hispanic world made use of genres currently considered "literary" in presenting their information, since, it must be recalled, journalism up to the late nineteenth century was less concerned with objectively communicating news than with self-expression, opinion, and ideological debate.

Even Lizardi's choice of the picaresque genre can be linked to his journalistic endeavor, not only because the picaresque novels and the early journalism of the sixteenth and seventeenth centuries have a common origin, nor just because the picaresque is an early form of *Bildungsroman,* but also, quite simply, because almost all journalists of the period in Spain and Spanish America frequently used pseudonyms that evoked lower-class, marginal, or regional characters: El Payo del Rosario, Fígaro, El Pobrecito Hablador, El Curioso Parlante, El Bachiller Cantaclaro, El Gíbaro de Caguas, among others. Early-nineteenth-century journalists, including the *costumbristas,* often preferred to assume the protective persona of the country bumpkin or of the lazy, disinterested spectator when writing their polemical or critical articles. Although Lizardi's pseudonym was the decidedly *un*-picaresque "El Pensador Mexicano," "El Periquillo Sarniento" would not have been inappropriate, either as a pseudonym or as the title of one of the polemical pamphlets Lizardi loved to write (one of Lizardi's last pamphlets was entitled *La Victoria del Perico*). Suffice it to say that on every level it is almost impossible to distinguish the discourse of *El Periquillo Sarniento* from that of the newspapers and gazettes of its day.

Nevertheless, Lizardi insists on *El Periquillo's* fictional nature, on its presumed difference from the journalism he was forbidden to write. *El Periquillo Sarniento* appears to confirm perfectly, in the Spanish American environment, the thesis presented by Lennard Davis with regard to journalism and the origins of the English novel. Davis argues that

the novel's fictionality is a ploy to mask the genuine ideological, reportorial commentative function of the novel. . . . Novels came about partly as a complex reaction to the laws, statutes, and legal decisions that were aimed at restricting journalism. Therefore, novels may be seen as tangible forms of highly encoded and profoundly reflexive defenses against authority and power. The novel embodies the contradictory qualities of rebellion and conformity, of criminality and morality, of criticism and approbation of society, and so on. (pp. 213, 222)

This thesis, although somewhat circular when applied to all novels in all epochs, describes perfectly what Lizardi did in early nineteenth-century Mexico. When Lizardi insisted that his text is an "obra romancesca," a work of narrative fiction, it was because his Spanish American readers already had a commonly accepted notion of what such a work must be like. Indeed, had Spanish-American Colonial readers (including the government censors) not had a certain idea of what a novel looked like in their age, Lizardi's whole strategy would have failed. The narrator explicitly states in his prologue that his work "may be useful to those young men who lack, perhaps, better works from which to learn, or also to certain young (and not so young) men who are fond of reading little novels and comedies [*que sean amigos de leer novelitas y comedias*]" (p. 5).

In writing *El Periquillo*, Lizardi made use of the generic differentiation that had already taken place between the novel and other forms of narrative. *El Periquillo* mimics a novel not merely because Lizardi labels it as one, but because it incorporates characters, situations, and figures derived from the most easily recognizable novelistic genre of the day, the picaresque. *El Periquillo* is a simulation in the very precise sense Severo Sarduy gives to this term in the passage that serves as my epigraph: It is not a copy, but a work that uses the observer's (the reader's) position to produce an imposture. Lizardi's readers expected a novel to provide them with certain themes, characters, and situations, and he gave them what they expected. But he did more; he tapped into a deeper level: that of rhetoric, a level in which the discourses of journalism and narrative fiction remain perpetually undifferentiated and undifferentiable (see the discussion in Chapter 1). It is at this level, in the murky no-man's-land of figural language shared by all discourses, that Lizardi was able to inject the substance of his journalistic writings into the mold of a picaresque tale. Lizardi's journalism, let us recall, was one of opinion and debate; in *El Periquillo*, his opinions could be expressed as those of the fictional characters, with the layers of character, plot, and situation to shield Lizardi from his censors. Curiously, however, like Periquillo himself, Lizardi went too far in his imposture. He was easily uncovered by the censor when he tried to bring into the last volume of his novel the highly charged and controversial subject of slavery: The censor then forbade that section's publication, and subscribers to the first edition of *El Periquillo* never got to read about the *pícaro*'s conversion to an upstanding citizen and a writer.

There is considerable irony in the realization that Spanish America's first self-proclaimed novel was actually a covert form of journalism, a pamphlet "in drag," passing itself off as a work of narrative fiction. To understand the oddity of Lizardi's situation, one need only imagine Thomas Paine (who, admittedly, was politically more radical than Lizardi) being forced to recast *Common Sense* (1776) as a short novel. Or better still, one need only recall the numerous instances in which nineteenth- and twentieth-century works of narrative fiction have presented themselves as their opposite: as journalism, autobiography, or history. Clearly, *El Periquillo* cannot be considered the "origin" of the modern Spanish American novel, whose roots go back to Colonial works such as Sigüenza y Góngora's *Los infortunios de Alonso Ramírez* (1690) and Carrió de la Vandera's *Lazarillo de ciegos caminantes* (1773). The facts of literary history plainly show that the novel has been created and re-created in Spanish America many times in different places. If *El Periquillo Sarniento* inaugurates anything, it is, I would argue, an increased awareness and strategic use in Spanish American writings of the tropological nature of discourses; a figural nature that allows the same discourse to be read as various, radically different – indeed sometimes antithetical – genres: pamphlet/novel, history/allegory, autobiography/fiction, etc. *El Periquillo* opens a tradition of discursive (dis)simulation in which journalism, because of its own protean nature, plays a key role. Henceforth, journalism was to be inscribed into virtually all major Spanish American works of narrative fiction as part of their strategy of textual (dis)simulation, of deliberately blurring discursive boundaries. After *El Periquillo,* we find in Spanish American narrative fiction simultaneous claims of truthfulness and verifiability and of utter fictionality, claims that mark this narrative's constant oscillation between journalistic and fictional discourses.

But the rich ideological implications of journalistic discourse ensure that it is not limited to the function of a mere disguise. In modern Spanish American narrative journalistic discourse plays a broader role: It is a source of themes, topics, terminology, and formal principles sometimes adopted and sometimes critiqued, but never ignored. To its practitioners, journalism is furthermore – to use a metaphor dear to nineteenth-century philologists (Said, pp. 123–48) – a laboratory in which the semiological and rhetorical secrets of narrative are systematically demystified and displayed, as language is taken down from its literary pedestal and turned into merchandise (see Chapter 5). To put it simplistically, journalistic discourse teaches writers about writing. Arguably, journalism democratizes writing, not only by broadening readership in general, but also by giving a greater number of would-be writers access to a knowledge about rhetoric that was once the exclusive province of the university and the academies. But, more radically still, journalistic discourse deflated forever – as did the inquiries of early nineteenth-century philologists (Foucault, *The Order of Things*, pp. 290–300) – the notion of language's divine origin; henceforth, language would be an all-too-human phenomenon, subject, as Nietzsche's well-known metaphor of the coin suggests (*Philosophenbuch*, pp. 180–2), to semiotic and economic evaluation and devaluation.

An ongoing and evolving entity, journalistic discourse is, as stated in Chapter 1, a vehicle of cultural change and socioeconomic modernization. Journalistic discourse gives modern Spanish American narrative its modernity, by injecting modernity's radical critique of values and principles, its constant return to the fundamentals of a discourse or discipline, into this narrative. Since *El Periquillo*, journalism has become the main auxiliary to Spanish American narrative's critical projects, which in some cases may be social or ideological, and in others more narrowly aesthetic in focus. In founding narrative works of nineteenth-century culture, such as Sarmiento's *Facundo* (1845), Palma's *Tradiciones peruanas* (1872–1910), and the turn-of-the-century Modernist chronicles, journalistic discourse is a growing and ever more powerful presence as well as a versatile critical instrument with which Spanish American writers attempt to pry open the secrets of national identity and of literature itself.

3
Sarmiento and sensationalist journalism: *Facundo* as crime story

> *If the reader is bored by these arguments, I will recount to him dreadful crimes.*
>
> Domingo F. Sarmiento, *Facundo* (1845)

> *And the novel? May we not pose the question of the novel — whose literary hegemony is achieved precisely in the nineteenth century — in the context of the age of discipline?*
>
> D. A. Miller, *The Novel and the Police* (1988)

It is already a hoary critical cliché to speak of Domingo Faustino Sarmiento's classic work, *Facundo, o Civilización y barbarie* (1845), as an unclassifiable, multifaceted, ageneric text. Critics have remarked for decades on the uneasy coexistence of heterogenous discourses in Sarmiento's text, such as those of natural and national history, politics, sociology, and narrative fiction. Carlos J. Alonso sagaciously observes that the very presence of the conjunction "*y*" ("and") in the work's subtitle (*Civilización y barbarie*) is an indication of the totalizing, amalgamating nature of this text, which tries forcibly to bring together seemingly disparate and incompatible concepts ("Civilización y barbarie," p. 257). But above and beyond its inner discursive diversity, *Facundo* achieves a certain unity as a complicated rhetorical performance designed to persuade its readers both of the evils of Juan Manuel de Rosas and of the possibility that the same Argentine reality that gave rise to the dictator may also produce his antithesis. As Noé Jitrik remarks, both the literariness and the apparent coherence of *Facundo* are in large part due to the rhetorical stratagems Sarmiento uses to convince his readers of the correctness of his views and the urgency of his message:

A fundamentally cumulative and spectacular intellect, Sarmiento tries less to demonstrate than to convince. It is easy to observe this finality: it is like a sort of pressure exerted upon the readers, covering them

42

with facts so that they will learn about something whose enormity or monstrosity they must necessarily condemn. If readers can realize by themselves that Facundo or Rosas are barbarous, Sarmiento reinforces such a realization by means of a chain of explanations that he presents as corroborations strengthened by verbal expressions of emotion and lyricism, and whose historical exactitude is not only variable but is sometimes totally eroded by the recognizably coercitive tone employed in the narration. History and sociology are turned by Sarmiento into instruments to achieve the goal of convincing his reading public. (pp. 11–12)

Originally a political pamphlet aimed to persuade and move public opinion, Sarmiento's work grew (monstrously?) into something that outlived its original intent. As early as 1845, the first anonymous reviewers of *Facundo* considered it "a sort of historical novel," remarking that Sarmiento was destined to be, "for the countries which he knows and studies, what [Washington] Irving and [James Fenimore] Cooper have been to the America on the other side of the Equator" (Verdevoye, p. 428). If Fernández de Lizardi's *El Periquillo Sarniento* was a pamphlet masquerading as a novel, Sarmiento's *Facundo* was a pamphlet that *became* a novel. And this was partly due, I would argue, to its links with journalism. *Facundo*'s links with literature, and specifically its novelistic character, are not only a consequence of its rhetorical, persuasive intention, but also of its use of journalistic discourse. One variety of that discourse that is particularly prominent in *Facundo*, but which has been consistently overlooked, is sensationalist journalism.

But what, exactly, is sensationalism in this context? *Webster's New World Dictionary* defines it as "the use of strongly emotional subject matter, or wildly dramatic style, language, or artistic expression, that is intended to shock, startle, thrill, excite, etc." Sensationalism also, as Mitchell Stephens reminds us, "appears to be a technique or style that is rooted somehow in the nature of the news . . . most news *is*, in an important sense, sensational: it is intended, in part, to arouse, to excite, often . . . to shock" (p. 2). Journalistic sensationalism is fundamentally connected to information and narration; it deals with events, not with opinions. It is true, of course, that the expression of an opinion in a certain context might be an inherently sensational event. Such was the case with the Spanish American independence-era pamphlets and journals, and they should be considered precursors of this mode. However, in the form it took in Europe and the United States, which is the one Sarmiento tried to import to Chile in the 1840s, journalistic sensationalism is essentially narrative: It tells a story, and the more lurid and unusual, the better.

In the field of journalism, sensationalism is an ancient and time-honored technique, dating as far back as the earliest medieval news-ballads, that was subsequently taken up in the printed newsbooks and broadsides of Renaissance Europe. The titles (or headlines) of such works are highly illustrative; among the many picturesque examples Mitchell Stephens cites are: *Du serpent ou dragon volant, grand et merveilleux, apparu & veu par un chacun, sur la ville de Paris* (France, 1579); *The crying Murther: Contayning the cruell and most horrible Butcher of Mr. Trat . . .* (England, 1637) (pp. 112–31). In Spanish America, precedents may be found in Christopher Columbus' 1493 letter announcing his discovery of "the Indies," with its descriptions of nude indigenous men and women, as well as in the many *relaciones* of the Conquest, with their often unbelievable accounts of pitched battles between a few Spaniards and "thousands" of Indians, and in gossipy and satirical chronicles such as Juan Rodríguez Freyle's *El Carnero* (1637). Indeed, the first known broadside (*hoja volante*) printed in the New World, which appeared in Mexico in 1542, contains a vivid and terrifying account of an earthquake that had taken place in Guatemala the year before (Henestroza and Castro, p. 11).

This last example reminds us that sensationalism can be of either content or style; events can be inherently sensational or they can be made to seem that way through rhetorical devices. Generally, however, journalistic sensationalism is concerned with events that engage the passions and feelings of the public in a personal, individual way. Although natural disasters, wars, and civil strife would seem to be inherently sensational and can indeed be reported in a sensationalist style, it is more common for sensationalist journalism to be concerned with events that touch the lives of specific, clearly identifiable individuals. Crimes of all sorts, bizarre or unusual occurrences (the sighting of a "flying dragon" in the skies over Paris in the sixteenth century, or a UFO in more recent times; the birth of a two-headed animal or human, etc.), and sexual scandals or the amorous misadventures of well-known people are the very stuff of sensationalist journalism.

Because of its interest in individuals and how they react to the events that disrupt or change their lives, sensationalist journalism tends to view events in a markedly theatrical manner, and its rhetoric is that of the melodrama. Indeed, sensationalism could be defined as the fusion of melodrama with factualism. The scandalous happenings and bloody crimes it usually reports are framed in a moralizing context in an attempt, however crude, to explore the workings of the human psyche. Sensationalism is almost unthinkable without some sort of implicit "psychology," some curiosity about why people act or react in given ways in specific contexts. Its exploration of motives and of plots (in every sense of the term) is also, of course, a common trait of fictional narrative. It would not be altogether irreverent or far-fetched to consider *Oedipus Rex* the prototype of this sort of journalism; if Sophocles' character has been seen by many as the first fictional detective or crime-solver, it is no less true that he was also a criminal of a sensational sort.[1] Like the *fait-divers* (or "human-interest story," of which more is said in Chapter 4), to which it is obliquely related, sensationalism constantly treads on the diffuse borderline between the journalistic and the literary discourses of its period.

Facundo, as is known, was first published as a *folletín* in the pages of the Chilean daily *El Progreso* from May 2 to June 21, 1845. Sarmiento's first venture into journalism was in the mold of the mercantile paper with the short-lived newspaper, *El Zonda,* which he founded in 1839 in his hometown of San Juan de la Frontera in western Argentina (Verdevoye, p. 14). Two years later, while living in exile in Chile, he wrote for that country's first daily, *El Mercurio* (founded in 1827 in Valparaíso), which was also predominantly mercantile. Shortly thereafter, he was hired, along with Vicente Fidel López, to be chief editor of *El Progreso.* Founded in 1842 in Santiago, Chile, by the Vial family, this was originally intended to be a political newspaper to further the aspiration of one family member, Manuel Camilo Vial, to the presidency of the republic (Silva, pp. 178, 180–2). Sarmiento was editor of *El Progreso* during two different periods: from its first appearance in 1842 to May 1843, and from March 1844 to October 1845 (Silva, p. 182). In recent years, scholars have stressed Sarmiento's role as a founding figure of modern Spanish-American journalism; a modernizer in journalism as in everything else, Sarmiento brought to the pages of *El Progreso* a whole suite of reforms that sought to increase and diversify the newspaper's informative content (Verdevoye, pp. 267–8). Despite its resemblance to the early mercantile newspapers, this daily was molded by Sarmiento into a different sort of publication, one that sought to combine the more modern "journalism of information" with the more traditional "journalism of opinion."

Sarmiento's modernizing impulse, along with his Romantic populism, which he showed in his well-known polemic with Andrés Bello in the pages of *El Mercurio* in 1842, also led him to adopt and adapt in *El Progreso* a very recent French innovation, the *roman-feuilleton* (serial novel), known as *"folletín"* in Spanish. In an 1845 article in *El Progreso*, he takes credit for having "inoculated" the Chilean press with "the virus of the 'feuilleton'" (Verdevoye, p. 268). It is not surprising that Sarmiento, who in 1839 founded a school for girls in San Juan, should have decided to include a *folletín* in the pages of *El Progreso*. Introduced in Paris in 1836 by two competing dailies, Emile de Girardin's *La Presse* and Armand Dutaq's *Le Siècle*, the *roman-feuilleton* was directed to a growing feminine readership (Bellanger et al. *Histoire générale de la presse française*, pp. 114–22). It was also, of course, meant to raise the newspapers' circulation, since its serial nature enticed readers to extend their subscriptions. However, most of the texts published under the rubric of the *folletín* in *El Progreso* were translations of French and English novels (from Balzac's *Père Goriot* to Bulwer-Lytton's *Rienzi*) and only one was a true serial – the archetype of the genre, Eugene Sue's *Les Mystères de Paris* (Garrels, p. 425, 436). Thus, as Elizabeth Garrels notes, the *folletín* in *El Progreso* did not follow the usual rules of the genre, since it consisted mostly of reprinted translations of texts that had been published originally as integral works, or that had already assumed a "fixed" format when *El Progreso* picked them up; there was none of the give-and-take with the reading public characteristic of the *roman-feuilleton* (p. 425). Although Sarmiento probably intended to use the *folletín* mostly as a device to keep subscriptions high, it also became a way to introduce his readers to the

Romantic aesthetic that he championed in his polemic with Bello, and to bring (it remains to be seen how deliberately) an element of sensationalism to his newspaper. Most of the texts serialized in the *folletín* had strong sensationalistic elements; this was, in fact, one reason they were so effective in helping to increase the newspapers' readership.

It is my contention that *Facundo*, the most enduring of Sarmiento's works, is imbued with the melodramatic rhetoric of journalistic sensationalism, one it shares, to be sure, with the *roman-feuilleton*, as well as with the crime stories that were the *feuilleton*'s main source of inspiration. This rhetoric gives *Facundo* its literariness and its novelistic qualities, but also keeps it in an inchoate state due to journalism's counterbalancing insistence on veracity and verifiability.

An undoubtedly partial but nonetheless revealing reading of *Facundo* would show it to be a variety of the crime story. The term "crime story" itself describes a rather large and diffuse category of texts in which journalism and fiction intersect. These include the popular Spanish crime ballads recounted in the *romances de ciego* and the *literatura de cordel*, the incipient sensationalist criminal reporting in the penny newspapers of the 1830s and 1840s, the *feuilleton* (the novels of Eugène Sue and Alexandre Dumas, *père*), and the English "Newgate novels" of Edward Bulwer-Lytton, Charles Dickens, and William Harrison Ainsworth.[2] Although *Facundo* does not closely resemble any of the above-mentioned forms in particular, it contains elements from all of them. Like the *romances de ciego*, it draws from the popular, oral tradition for information on the life of Facundo Quiroga, and thus turns him into a quasi-legendary outlaw figure similar to the bandits glorified in the *literatura de cordel*.[3] Like sensationalist crime journalism (such as that pioneered by James Gordon Bennett in the *New York Herald* in 1836), it corroborates facts through eyewitness accounts and personal knowledge of the "crime scene."[4] Like the *feuilleton*, it was originally published in serial form and makes deliberate use of suspense at certain points in the text (Garrels, p. 431). Finally, like the English Newgate novels, the text of *Facundo* attempts to explain the origins of a criminal career through an examination of the individual's social milieu and contains a "disciplinary" subtext that portrays the mechanisms of law and order in society in order to reform them (see Miller; more is said about this at the end of this chapter). In contrast, however, the melodramatic rhetoric found in *Facundo* is a discursive element present in all of these texts that springs inevitably from their popular, sensationalist nature. Clearly, *Facundo*'s link with a quasi-journalistic form like the crime story is one of the most important connections between its discourse and that of the nineteenth-century novel.

The structure and content of *Facundo* as it appeared in book form in the fall of 1845 are difficult to summarize, due to the highly digressive nature of the text; nevertheless, an attempt must be made in order to note the similarities and differences between Sarmiento's work and the genre of the crime story. The text is divided into fifteen chapters, along with an "Advertencia del autor" ("Author's Foreword") and an "Introducción" (of which more is said below). Chapters 1 to 3 present a panoramic view, couched in the terminology of natural history as exemplified by the work of Alexander von Humboldt (González Echevarría, "Redescubrimiento del mundo perdido," pp. 389–401), of the geographic milieu and its relationship to the social organization of Argentina. In Chapter 1, after writing on the geography of Argentina and on its cities, Sarmiento focuses his attention on the countryside and on the gaucho in particular. This continues in Chapter 2, where, after some general comments on the relationship between the Argentine landscape and the gauchos' customs, including their music (again following the example of early-nineteenth-century natural history), Sarmiento proposes a highly schematic social typology of the gauchos. He discerns among the gauchos four overlapping types that he considers representative of the gauchos' overall cultural peculiarity: the *rastreador,* or tracker, the *baqueano,* or scout, the *gaucho malo,* or outlaw, and the *cantor,* or singer. This typology, as can be seen, is not rigorous, nor is it always based on social criteria. Deliberately partial, it is apparently intended to serve as a description of the positive and negative elements in the gauchos' value system and as a prelude to the attributes of Facundo Quiroga. But it is also related to *Facundo*'s disciplinary subtext: It is not by chance that two of the types, the tracker and the scout, have frequently served in the army and the police (pp. 44–6).

Chapter 3 shows how life in the Argentine countryside, though apparently chaotic, follows a certain logic and constitutes a form of social order. Here Sarmiento introduces the main thesis of his book: that Argentina is constituted by two conflicting societies living side by side, "one Spanish, European, cultured, and the other barbarous, American, almost like that of the Indians" (p. 61). Chapter 4 further develops this basic contrast by studying the effects of the gaucho armies (*montoneras*), mobilized by the civil wars, upon the provinces and cities of the Argentine interior, such as Sarmiento's native San Juan. Not surprisingly, Sarmiento finds that whatever progress was made in establishing an urban, European-style civilization in the provinces has been rolled back by their "barbarization" (p. 71) at the hands of the military chieftains who have taken over.

It is not until Chapter 5 that Sarmiento begins his account of Facundo Quiroga's life, which forms the basis for the book's narrative. Chapter 5 covers Facundo's infancy and youth, Chapter 6 tells of his rise to power as a commander of the provincial armies, and Chapters 7 to 13 give an account of Facundo's participation in the civil wars and political struggles between Unitarians and Federalists, as well as of Facundo's assassination at Barranca-Yaco in 1835. Chapters 14 and 15 offer a summary of Juan Manuel de Rosas' rise to nearly absolute power after Facundo's death, a program of action against Rosas' dictatorship, and the measures to be taken by the new government to restore Argentina after the tyrant's fall.

The basic elements of the crime story can already be discerned in the pages of the "Introducción" to *Facundo*. Sarmiento begins with a truculent invocation that in style is reminiscent of a scene of necromancy from a Gothic novel or play, and in content of an autopsy or coroner's report: "Terrible shade of Facundo, I am going to evoke you, so that, shaking the blood-stained dust that covers your ashes, you will rise and explain the secret life and internal convulsions that tear the entrails of a noble people! You possess the secret: reveal it to us!" (p. 7). Sarmiento goes on to indicate that Facundo's "natural," artless violence and brutality were merely the prefiguration of the more systematic, artful, and total violence of the dictator Juan Manuel de Rosas. The latter, says Sarmiento, is an "Argentine

Sphinx" who "proposes to us the enigma of the political organization of the Republic," and, like the Theban Sphinx, is destined to die once that enigma is solved (p. 9). Implicit in this
assertion is that Sarmiento will be the Oedipus to Rosas' Sphinx.

The Oedipal scenario, as we have already remarked, is related to sensationalist journalism as well as to detective fiction.
Facundo is in many ways a piece of crime journalism, and as
such its discourse is similar to that of a detective novel. True to
Sarmiento's tendency toward antinomy and dualism, *Facundo*,
as a narrative, has two plots: The most obvious one is the story
of the life and times of Facundo Quiroga; but, set in an ambiguous position, both inside and outside the text (in the "Introducción," the author's notes, and the coda-like Chapters 14 and
15), as a sort of meta-plot, is also the story of Sarmiento's detec-
tivelike investigation into the murder of Facundo Quiroga. The
narrative thread of the text is propelled by a central mystery:
Who killed Facundo Quiroga? Or, to be more specific, since the
actual killers were caught and punished: Who ordered Facundo
killed? The text declares that it was the tyrant Juan Manuel de
Rosas, and to a great extent all the historical and geographical
digressions in *Facundo* are ancillary to Sarmiento's task of
"building a case" against Rosas for this particular murder as
well as for his acts of tyranny.[5]

Sarmiento's decision to investigate and narrate the life and
death of Facundo Quiroga is evidently a strategic one since,
through it, he is able to strike at Rosas in a way that does not
increase further the tyrant's reputation. Sarmiento is aware that
the literary representation of evil can give the impression that
evil is unconquerable. Rosas, he admits, is a "tyrant without
equal on earth today; . . . [who] is great indeed, to the glory
and shame of his fatherland" (p. 9); but, Sarmiento claims,
the totality of his crimes cannot yet be told, because "the last
page of this immoral biography has not yet been formed; the
cup is not yet full" (p. 15). Instead, Sarmiento concentrates on
Facundo Quiroga, and asks, "Who launched the *official* bullet
that cut short his career? Did it come from Buenos Aires or
from Córdoba? History will explain this arcanum" (p. 15; Sarmiento's emphasis). Like a good investigative reporter, Sarmiento knows that the detailed recounting of a specific crime or
scandal can be far more effective in mobilizing public opinion

against an adversary than a mere listing of that adversary's crimes.

Facundo's assassination provides Sarmiento with just such a crime. For Sarmiento, Facundo is both a criminal and a victim, a prototype of the *caudillo* and a tragic figure. He was "the purest example of the character of the Argentine civil wars; . . . the most American figure presented by the revolution . . . ; he made of local war a national, Argentine war, and triumphantly produced, after ten years of labors, devastations, and combat, the results that were reaped by his assassin" (p. 15). Facundo Quiroga is, for Sarmiento, original in every sense of the term. Following the classical providentialist notion of "The Great Chain of Being" that was resuscitated during the Victorian era, Sarmiento sees Facundo as the primitive and bestial, yet not unworthy, antecedent of a more powerful and complex entity like Rosas, and, ultimately, of Sarmiento himself (González Echevarría, "Redescubrimiento," p. 399). Furthermore, if Facundo's life helps to explain the origins of Rosas' brutal sway over his country, his death dramatizes Rosas' traitorous nature and serves as a reminder that "there is no honor among thieves."

But let us examine other details that make *Facundo* a crime story and display Sarmiento's use of the rhetoric of melodrama for sensationalist purposes. In Chapter 5, Sarmiento collects, retells, and interprets a large number of anecdotes concerning Facundo's early years. Facundo's rebellious, criminal career began early in life when he hit his teacher after being punished in school for making mistakes (p. 82). His first killing was of one Jorge Peña, whom he shot during a gambling dispute (p. 82). Gambling was one of Facundo's most constant vices; because of it, he abandoned his rural middle-class origins and his studies and became a farmhand, building wall fences for the farms of the region. He was also pathologically cruel, striking out at anyone who happened to be near him when he was enraged (pp. 83, 87). He was reported to have slapped his father in the face for refusing to give him money, and later tried to burn down his parents' house while they were sleeping inside (p. 84). All in all, Facundo is worthy of his epithet, *El Tigre de los Llanos* (The Tiger of the Plains), derived from the highly symbolic anecdote with which Sarmiento begins this chapter.[6] Sarmiento's description of Facundo, influenced by the pseudoscientific beliefs in phrenology and physiognomy that were common at the time, also stresses the latter's physical resemblance to a tiger:

There are, in fact, as is proved by phrenology and comparative anatomy, relations between external forms and moral qualities, between the countenance of a man and that of some animal whose disposition resembles his own. . . . Facundo was . . . of short and sturdy build; his broad shoulders and short neck supported a well-formed head covered with very thick hair, black and curly. His somewhat oval face was half-buried in a dense forest of hair and an equally thick black, curly beard, rising to his cheekbones, which by their prominence showed his firm and tenacious will. His black and fiery eyes, shadowed by thick eyebrows, occasioned an involuntary sense of terror in those on whom they chanced to fall. Facundo's glance was never direct, and whether from habit, intention, or with the design of making himself always fearsome, he always kept his head bent down, to look at one from under his eyebrows, like the Ali Pasha of Monvoisin. . . . As to the rest, his features were regular, and the pale olive of his features harmonized well with the dense shadows that surrounded it. . . . The formation of his head showed, notwithstanding this shaggy covering, the peculiar organization of a man born to rule. Quiroga possessed those natural qualities that converted the student of Brienne into the genius of France, and the obscure Mameluke who fought with the French at the Pyramids, into the Viceroy of Egypt. Such natures develop according to the society in which they originate: sublime and classical, so to speak, in some places they lead civilized mankind; elsewhere, terrible, bloodthirsty, and evil, they are its scourge, its disgrace. (p. 81)

As Roberto González Echevarría has pointed out, Facundo's actions are motivated by a surfeit of vitality, of life-energy. This vital excess, like the classical *hybris*, propels Facundo in his violent rise to power and leads him to his fatal and tragic end at Barranca-Yaco (p. 406). Indeed, Facundo, whatever his real attributes may have been, exists in Sarmiento's text – to use Peter Brook's formulation – in "the mode of excess." Like the "great men" of Hegel and Carlyle, Facundo is larger than life; all his gestures are subject to magnification, to expansion, like his bid (which no one dared contest) for the tithes of La Rioja province: "I give two thousand pesos and one more than the best bid" (p. 97). A creature of extremes, Facundo is excessive in both the good and the bad: His cruelty, when aroused, can lead to mass execution and torture; his generosity is unpredictable and overwhelming, as seen in his treatment of General Alvarado (p. 151). Facundo's excessive nature is explained by Sarmiento in Chapters 1 and 2 as an emanation of the overabundance and grandeur of American Nature, but, going beyond Sarmiento's romantic ideology, we can see that it is also an effect of representation due to Sarmiento's use of sensationalism and the rhetoric of melodrama. As a character in the narrative, Facundo is excessive in part because the narrative is itself exaggerated and melodramatic.

Melodrama, Peter Brooks notes, arises from an interpretative impulse that seeks to divine the ultimate causes of seemingly chaotic real-world events.[7] This impulse produces a discourse which, in Brooks' trenchant formulation, seeks

to express all. . . . Nothing is spared because nothing is left unsaid; the characters stand on stage and utter the unspeakable, give voice to their deepest feelings, dramatize through their heightened and polarized words and gestures the whole lesson of their relationship. They assume primary psychic roles, father, mother, child, and express basic psychic conditions. Life tends, in this fiction, towards ever more concentrated and totally expressive gestures and statements. (p. 4)

Particularly relevant to *Facundo* is Brooks' observation that Balzac's novels are more successful as melodramas than his earlier theatrical experiments "partly because he can offer a view of all that goes on, in the words of René Guise, 'behind the drama offered to the spectators'; he can perform its 'autopsy'" (p. 111). Nevertheless, drama remains an integral part of Balzac's novelistic writing, to the extent that his novels abound in *tableaux*, key scenes in which the characters confront each other and bring their conflicts into the open (p. 112).

Sarmiento's text, we will recall, offers itself as an "autopsy" of sorts, as an attempt to divine the truth about Argentine history and to understand the forces that power Argentina's historical drama through a sort of Gothic necromancy performed on Facundo Quiroga's dead body. Sarmiento's rhetoric, furthermore, abounds in violent antitheses, such as the one that presides over the text as a whole: Civilization/Barbarism. *Tableaux* abound in this text, but with a significant difference from those in Balzac: although they constitute highly dramatic moments, they use little dialogue, and what is important remains unsaid

by the characters (in spite of the expressiveness of their gestures, which Sarmiento describes). A good example is the story
of Facundo's brutal courtship of Severa Villafañe in Chapter 10.

Severa's tale is narrated by Sarmiento in a falsely ironic tone
that is intended to disarm its critics. From the beginning, Sarmiento shows his awareness of the story's resemblance to "a
pitiful romance; a fairy tale in which the loveliest princess is a
wandering fugitive, sometimes disguised as a shepherdess,
sometimes begging a morsel of bread, or for protection from a
frightful giant, – a cruel Bluebeard" (p. 149). Near the story's
end, Sarmiento again exclaims with irony, "Isn't this a pretty
romance?" (p. 150). But this irony is merely a ploy, a kind of
Hegelian double negation that in the end reaffirms the story's
shocking and sensational nature by pretending to present it
free from rhetorical artifice. The rhetorical artifice is precisely
the irony with which Severa's tale is narrated; moreover, the
content of the anecdote is sufficiently melodramatic in and of
itself:

For whole years Severa resisted. At one time she came close to being
poisoned with a dried fig by her tiger; at another, Quiroga, in a fit of
desperation, tried to poison himself with opium. Once she escaped
with difficulty from the hands of some of his assistants, who were
going to spread-eagle her against a wall to offend her modesty, and
again she was surprised in her own courtyard by Quiroga, who seized
her by the arm, beat her until she was bathed in blood, then threw her
upon the ground and kicked in her skull with the heel of his boot. (p.
149)

The story culminates in a highly theatrical scene of recognition,
when, after finding refuge for two years in a convent in Cata-
marca, Severa is coincidentally discovered by Facundo, and,
upon seeing him, faints (p. 150). Despite the profusion of *tableaux* in this brief narrative, there is no dialogue, and seemingly
no opportunity for the characters to indulge in a melodramatic
revelation of motives through an exchange of words, in the
manner of Balzac. However, if the characters remain silent,
the narrator certainly does not, and it is he who gives voice to
"the unspeakable" (in Brooks' formulation) by means of the
falsely ironic expressions quoted above, as well as by more conventionally melodramatic exclamations such as: "Good God!

Isn't there anyone who can come to the aid of this poor girl? Has she no relatives? No friends?" (pp. 149–50).

Another example of melodramatic technique occurs in Chapter 12, when Facundo enters Tucumán amid a campaign of terror that includes public executions. Antithesis is prevalent in this passage, but here the violent contrasts and polarities are kept muted until the end in order to shock and surprise the readers. Sarmiento begins by describing, in unusually vivid and precious language, the natural environment of Tucumán, calling it "the Eden of America, without rival in all the earth" (pp. 174–5). He dwells at length on the variety of trees and flowers in that province, and in a conventionally smooth metaphorical shift, proceeds to speak about the women of Tucumán:

The city is surrounded for many leagues by a forest of orange-trees, rounded to about the same height, so as to form a vast canopy supported by millions of smooth columns. The rays of the torrid sun have never looked upon the scenes which are enacted upon the carpet of green that covers the earth beneath this immense roof. And what scenes! The young girls of Tucumán pass the Sundays in those limitless galleries. Each family chooses a convenient place. If it is Autumn, the oranges that fell to the ground are swept aside, or else couples dance over the thick carpet of orange blossoms, intoxicated with the perfume of the flowers and the melodious and sad songs accompanied by the guitars. Do you perhaps believe this description to be copied from the *Arabian Nights,* or other Eastern-style fairy tales? Hasten instead to imagine what I do not say about the voluptuousness and beauty of the women born under a fiery sky, who recline languorously to softly sleep their siesta under the shade of the myrtles and laurels, drunk on such scents as would bring asphyxia upon one unaccustomed to the atmosphere. (pp. 175–6)

Once again Sarmiento creates a *tableau,* and again the language is one of extremes, although this time they are positive in sign (extreme beauty, suffocating perfumes, intoxication). The ironic allusion to the *Arabian Nights* only serves to underscore the hyperbolic exoticism of this passage. Into this idyllic scene enters Facundo, who is in this case compared with a lion who has caught a squirrel (Tucumán) in its paws (p. 176). In typical Romantic fashion, the landscape seems to affect Facundo, and his behavior is in accord with the serenity and sweetness of the environment. As he sits incongruously meditating under the orange-trees, a delegation of young women from the city approaches him timidly to implore his mercy for the lives of the army officers who are going to be shot. Facundo receives the young women with unexpected courtesy and interest. Sarmiento, like a dramatist giving stage directions, carefully portrays all the nuances of his character's behavior: the shyness and coquetry of the women, Facundo's surprising urbanity as he engages them in lengthy conversation about their families and daily lives. Thus, the narration's climax is even more shocking when Facundo quietly asks the women: "Do you hear those shots?" (p. 176).

As in the story of Severa, it is the narrator who reveals and underscores the terrifying implication of this phrase, with his exclamation: "It is too late! They have been shot! A cry of horror arose from that choir of angels, who dispersed like a flock of doves pursued by a falcon" (p. 176). This is followed by a brutally antithetical description of the shootings: "Thirty-three officers from the rank of colonel downward, drawn up in the town square, totally naked, received standing up the mortal volley" (p. 176).

These two brief examples suffice to show how Sarmiento's writing in *Facundo* is, in Noé Jitrik's phrase, "cumulative and spectacular" indeed. It is important to stress, however, that the rhetoric of melodrama in this text is closely allied to a historiographic and journalistic insistence on verifiability: This is the key to *Facundo*'s effectiveness as a sensationalist work. Sensationalism, as we said earlier, is melodrama allied to facts; factualism is an intrinsic component of sensationalism. It is from its insistence on factuality, as much as from its use of melodrama, that sensationalism derives much of its impact. The documentary nature of *Facundo* is therefore not incongruent with its sensationalist aims. And yet, the melodramatic treatment to which it subjects "the facts" leaves Sarmiento's work open to charges of fictionalization.

Needless to say, unlike Fernández de Lizardi and *El Periquillo Sarniento* in Mexico almost thirty years earlier, Sarmiento regarded any consideration of *Facundo* as fiction as a danger to his work, since this would undermine the text's nature as a political pamphlet (in this context, the anonymous reviewer I quoted at the beginning paid Sarmiento an ambiguous compliment in calling his text an "historical novel"). That is why Sarmiento insisted in his "Introducción" on the thoroughness of his fact-gathering, even while admitting that there might be "inexactitudes" in the writing of his work and asking his readers to point these out to him (p. 16). After his friend Valentín Alsina obliged him in 1846 with a lengthy list of mistakes he had observed in the first edition of *Facundo*, Sarmiento's public attitude toward his text's veracity became much more humble and self-critical, as can be seen in the "Carta-prólogo" to the 1851 edition. It is interesting to note, however, that as early as December 1845, in a letter to General José María Paz, Sarmiento cavalierly referred to *Facundo* as an "improvised work, full of sometimes deliberate inexactitudes" (p. 3, note 2). This does not mean that Sarmiento intended to write a work of fiction, but it does point to *Facundo*'s primarily sensationalistic and propagandistic nature. The *appearance* of factualism was important, even though Sarmiento might take liberties with the facts.

Another double-faced aspect of *Facundo* that underlines its shared links with both the journalism and narrative fiction of its day is the disciplinary subtext that is present in crime reporting as well as in such works of early-nineteenth-century fiction as the Newgate novels. Following the ideas of Michel Foucault in *Surveiller et punir* (1975), D. A. Miller has argued that the evolution of the novel during the nineteenth century resulted in texts that incorporated the disciplinary strategies that were being developed in Western society at that time (pp. 1–32). Sarmiento's *Facundo* shares this process, but in a topsy-turvy fashion, due to the peculiar circumstances of its writing. I say "topsy-turvy" because – unlike the examples from the novels of Wilkie Collins, Dickens, and Trollope adduced by Miller, or from Lizardi's picaresque *El Periquillo Sarniento*, in which the disciplinary strategies of society are marshalled against individuals who deviate from the norms and are therefore branded as "criminals" – in *Facundo* it is the individual, Sarmiento, who must struggle to police and bring to justice whole sectors of Argentine society that have been corrupted and "criminalized" by Rosas.

It is true, as Miller points out regarding *David Copperfield*, that in many nineteenth-century novels, and in works such as *Facundo*, we find a "dreary pattern in which the subject constitutes himself 'against' discipline by assuming that discipline in his own name" (p. 220). In any case, *Facundo*, as befits a textual product of a civil war, brings such a pattern out into the open by exposing the arbitrariness that underlies the relation between ethics, power, and the law. Quiroga and Rosas, despite their "outlaw" origins, imposed their own version of "discipline" upon a war-torn land – a version that turns Sarmiento into an "outlaw." Who shall judge? Sarmiento? God? The "civilized countries" such as France, England, and the United States (Sarmiento, pp. 9–15, 236–7)? Sarmiento obviously relies greatly for support on the force of public opinion in Europe and the United States as well as on a providentialist view of history as "progress" (pp. 13, 236–7). Nevertheless, in the end it comes down to a conflict of wills: "One does not renounce such a grand future, such an elevated mission, because of such an accumulation of contradictions and difficulties: difficulties can be overcome, and contradictions are dissolved by contradicting them!" (p. 14). For Sarmiento, contradictions are to be willfully erased by means of contra-*diction*, the continuous and systematic insistence on one's principles.

As part of his strategy of contra-*diction*, Sarmiento seeks to show how Argentine society, though capable of producing tyrants such as Quiroga and Rosas, who bend discipline to their own purposes (as in Rosas' forcing everyone to wear red ribbons with the slogan "Death to the savage Unitarists," p. 206), also generates principles of order that can be harnessed for better purposes. This explains, as mentioned earlier, his curious typology of the gauchos in Chapter 2. Two of the types – the tracker and the scout – are associated with discipline, with the army and the police (pp. 44–6); the other two – the outlaw and the singer – with delinquency and freedom from the law (pp. 47–9). The binary opposition suggested in this scheme tends to collapse as soon as each of the types is scrutinized and compared with the others: The tremendous powers of observation, memory, and induction of the tracker, as well as the incredibly detailed knowledge of the landscape possessed by the scout, are shared to a certain degree by the outlaw and the singer. One general characteristic that unites these four types is their possession of what, following Miller, we may call *supervision:*

Detective fiction is . . . always implicitly punning on the detective's brilliant *super-vision* and the police *supervision* that it embodies. His intervention marks an explicit bringing-under-surveillance of the entire world of the narrative. As such, it can be alarming. When Poe's Dupin reads his sidekick's mind in "The Murders in the Rue Morgue"; when, after a half-hour's sniffing about the scene of *L'affaire Lerouge*, Emile Gaboriau's Père Tabaret announces how and when the murder was committed as well as offers a physical description of the murderer; when Sherlock Holmes deduces a man's moral and economic history from his hat in "The Adventure of the Blue Carbuncle" – these prodigies are greeted as though they opened up the fearful prospect of an absolute surveillance under which everything would be known, incriminated, policed. (p. 35)

The *super-vision* of the tracker (who can see traces no one else can perceive, p. 44), of the scout (who holds in his mind a detailed map of the territory, p. 45), of the outlaw (who remembers the characteristics of every individual horse in the pampas, pp. 47–8), or of the singer (who re-collects the history of the nation in his songs, p. 48), point to a pervasive concern in *Facundo* with panoptism, with a totalizing vision, and its relation to power.[8] Rosas' nearly absolute control over Argentina, according to Sarmiento, is based largely on his institution of a mechanism of universal vigilance. In one of the many striking passages that can be quoted in this regard, Sarmiento compares Rosas' technique of governing with the administration of a ranch:

The parish festivities, which all the neighbors are compelled to attend, are an imitation of the *branding* of the cattle; the *red ribbon* he sticks onto every man, woman, or child, is the *brand* by which the ranch owner recognizes his cattle; the throat-cutting, instituted as the means of public execution, derives from the way cattle are slaughtered in the countryside; the imprisonment without cause of hundreds of citizens for years on end, is like the round-up with which cattle are made docile by herding them daily into the corrals; the beatings in the streets, the *Mazorca*, the massacres, are just other means of *taming* the *city*, leaving it like the most tame and orderly cattle that are known. (p. 211; italics in original)

Sarmiento's contra-*diction* to this vigilance is to propose a countervigilance of his own, through the medium of the press, of journalism. If Rosas can submit Argentina to his powerful vigilance, then from the pages of *El Progreso*, in the safe haven of Chile, Sarmiento can subject him to the same panoptic scrutiny. In a highly melodramatic direct address to Rosas in Chapter 15, Sarmiento exclaims:

Has he [Rosas] chained the Press and gagged the minds so that the interests of the country are not discussed, so that there is no education, so that his horrendous crimes, whose frightfulness makes them incredible, are not revealed? Fool! What have you done? The cries you wish to stifle by cutting throats, so that the voice escapes through the wound and not the lips, today resound to the ends of the earth. The presses of Europe and America call you constantly "the execrable Nero," "the brutal tyrant." All your crimes have been told; your victims find supporters and sympathy everywhere, and avenging cries reach your ears. The whole European press today discusses Argentine interests as if they were their own, and the name of Argentina, to your dishonor, is on the lips of every civilized people. Press discussion today is everywhere, and to oppose truth to your infamous *Gazette* there are a hundred dailies which, from Paris and London, Brazil and Chile, Montevideo and Bolivia, combat you and publish your wrongdoings. (p. 236)

It is undoubtedly risky to advance claims of precedence for any one of the many discourses that contribute to the long-lasting potency of Sarmiento's *Facundo,* but if there is any discourse that comes closest to subsuming all others in this text, it is that of sensationalist journalism. Any attempt to explain *Facundo* solely on the basis of biography, or of national or natural history, of sociology, or even of fiction, falls short of accounting for all or most aspects of the text. Although sensationalist journalism does not do so either, it does provide, I would argue, the broader discursive and generic framework within which Sarmiento's work was conceived. Sarmiento's intentions in writing *Facundo* were clear from the beginning: It was an attempt to strike a blow against Rosas by means of journalism. To do this, Sarmiento made use of the resources of sensationalism, with which he was acquainted through his experience as a journalist. Furthermore, his use of melodramatic rhetoric, allied to a choice of bizarre and violent but verifiable incidents in his narration, along with a metaplot derived from the crime story, not only transformed *Facundo* into a work of sensationalist journalism, but also contributed to providing the text with an appearance of homogeneity and narrative flow that linked it to the nineteenth-century novelistic tradition.

Such an impression of homogeneity also derived from Sarmiento's particular way of using the rhetoric of melodrama; instead of creating *tableaux* and allowing his characters to voice the deep polar oppositions they represented, Sarmiento assumed this function himself, oratorically upstaging his characters and becoming the principal player in his text. In this, he resembled the founder of modern journalistic investigation, the American James Gordon Bennett, whose path-breaking "on-the-spot" crime reporting during the 1830s was accompanied by a good deal of hyperbole and unabashed self-promotion (Stephens, pp. 242–8). In the course of his narrative, Sarmiento's voice assumes all the personae suggested in his typology of the gaucho: Tracker, Scout, Outlaw, and, of course, Singer of his country's history.[9] But perhaps the deadliest and most effective persona, in his struggle against Rosas, is that of the Journalist.

4

Journalism versus genealogy:
Ricardo Palma's *Tradiciones peruanas*

The tradición is not so much history as folk narrative, and,
as you know, common folk are the biggest liars. People have
taken a liking to [my tradiciones] not because they contain
much truth, but because they reveal the spirit and expression
of the multitudes.

Ricardo Palma, letter to Alberto Larco Herrera
(1907)

The above quote would seem at first to be only one of many
such expressions of Romantic populism that can be found in
Ricardo Palma's works, as well as in virtually all writers of the
Romantic period in Europe and America.[1] But in Palma's case,
such expressions are justified by his undeniable popularity as
an author, both in Peru and in the rest of the Spanish-speaking
world. Supported by an immense readership, by a "people"
who had "taken a liking" to his *Tradiciones peruanas*, Palma felt
he could faithfully voice their concerns and speak for them, in
their name. It should be remembered, however, that the "people" to whom Palma refers in the quote above were not the
same ones who read the *Tradiciones;* Palma's texts were refined
literary products, destined to be read by members of the Peruvian elite, and altogether inaccessible to the majority of the
Spanish American populace who, then as now, were illiterate.
José Carlos Mariátegui's observations on Palma's class origins,
and its effect on the writing of his *Tradiciones,* are still valid:

Palma belongs to a middle-class elite which, by a complex combination of historical circumstances, was not permitted to turn into a bourgeoisie. Like this composite, larval class, Palma nursed a latent resent-
ment against the oldtime, reactionary aristocracy. The satire of the
Tradiciones frequently sinks its sharp teeth into the men of the republic. But in contrast to the reactionary satire of Felipe Pardo y Aliaga, it
does not attack the republic itself. Palma, together with the demos in
Lima, is conquered by the anti-oligarchical oratory of Piérola. And,

above all, he remains faithful to the liberal ideology of independence. (p. 199)

There is no doubt that both Palma's populism and his popularity are due to his liberal ideology, regardless of the fact that, by virtue of a superficial reading, his writings also achieved favor among the conservative sectors of Peruvian society. But another explanation for the populism evident in the text of the *Tradiciones* and for their broad acceptance among Spanish-speaking readers in the nineteenth century resides in the link between the *Tradiciones* and journalism. In his *Tradiciones peruanas* Palma uses many of the resources provided by the journalistic rhetoric of his age (particularly of satirical journalism and the *fait-divers*), not only with the exclusively literary aim of producing a new narrative genre, but also with the extraliterary purpose of criticizing and deconstructing the genealogical framework that underlies nineteenth-century historicism. It was upon this framework that, because of the lack of a strong bourgeoisie, according to Mariátegui, the "oldtime, reactionary aristocracy" of Peru founded its claims to authority and dominion over the institutions of the republic.

No exploration of the links between journalism and the *Tradiciones* can proceed very far without facing the question of the genre to which the *Tradiciones* belong. As with many other products of Romantic literature, the generic nature of the *Tradiciones* is extremely problematic. The concept of "genre" itself, since its origins in antiquity, appears shrouded in biologistic and genealogical presuppositions that the literary ideology of Romanticism stressed even further, and that run counter to the very nature of the *Tradiciones*.[2] The *Tradiciones peruanas* are antigenealogical, and therefore antigeneric, texts. Not essay, nor short story, nor essay on manners, nor legend, Palma's *tradición* is itself a product of that "Neither-Nor criticism" ("critique Ni-Ni"), of petit bourgeois and liberal origins, described by Roland Barthes in his *Mythologies* (1957):

We are dealing here with a mechanism based on a double exclusion largely pertaining to this enumerative mania which we have already come across several times, and which I thought I could broadly define as a petit-bourgeois trait. One reckons all the methods with scales, one piles them up on each side as one thinks best, so as to appear oneself as an imponderable arbiter endowed with a spirituality which is ideal and thereby *just,* like the beam which is the judge in the weighing. (p. 81)

(Of course, in Palma's time and place, such a style of critical thinking was still a politically radical gesture and not the conservative stratagem that Barthes is denouncing.) Palma himself, in one of his many (and always unsatisfactory) definitions of the *tradición,* presented it as a genre that was halfway between historiography and narrative fiction, as a sort of "third way" between the stumbling blocks of historical veracity and the imaginative demands of fiction:

> What resulted from my lucubrations on the best way to popularize historical events was the intimate belief that the writer should give more importance to the form than to the facts themselves (such is Uncle Antón's Creed). The form must be light and gay like castanets, and if the story leaves the reader unsatisfied, we will have awakened his curiosity, forcing him to look in conscientious history books for however much or little he wishes to know as a complement to the thimbleful of honey we have given him to taste with a more or less quick and humoristic narration. An austere style in a *tradición* would fit as much as a *magnificat* at matins; in other words, it wouldn't be proper. Such was the origin of my *Tradiciones,* and blessed be the hour when, prompted by a feeling of Americanism, I began to reflect on the form – partly artistic, partly verbose – that was most suitable for them.[3]

Synthetic definitions such as Robert Bazin's, who argues that "romantic legend + essay on manners + purism (*casticismo*) = *tradición*" (p. 231), are attempts to impose coherence upon a "genre" (so to speak) that tends to question such attempts at synthesis. I find more convincing the observations of Alberto Escobar, who, even as he attempts to find an underlying generic coherence to the *tradición,* also takes note of the diverse and contradictory impulses that converge in Palma's work:

> If, upon reading Palma, we judge him only as someone who evokes our past, we are then omitting his very profound notion of actuality; if we take him to be a Hispanist, we are hiding his localist inspiration and his felicitous expression – in both form and content – of a Peruvian spirit; if we appreciate him only as a defender of literary nationalism, we lose sight of his continental preoccupations and his longing for a common Hispanic heritage, which, oddly enough, led him to disagree with Spanish academicians. If we wanted to explain his work in political terms, we would diminish his prodigious task of constructing a style that recreates a many-sided reality. (p. 113)

In his meticulous analysis of the stylistic modifications Palma made in his early *tradición* titled "Mauro Cordato" until it was transformed into "El mejor amigo . . . , un perro," Escobar shows that the "genre" of the *tradición* is not constituted by means of the *addition* of diverse elements, but by their *subtraction*. Palma excludes from the first version of his tale all those elements that can be attributed to the genres mentioned by Bazin, and replaces them with others that do not derive from the literary tradition but from journalism. For the moment, a significant indication of that critical negativity on which Palma's *tradición* is founded is the frequent presence, in his mature style, of the "asseveration by the exclusion of opposites." As Escobar notes, "instead of categorical statements, Palma prefers the suggestive statement that, eliminating its opposite, leaves some margin to the imagination. For example: 'the Pearl no longer had an orient;' 'myself not being yet an old man;' 'her husband was no potentate'" (p. 95).

Justifiably, Escobar has also seen in this and other stylistic traits of the *Tradiciones* an attempt by Palma to evoke orality – the flow of colloquial speech. But the orality of Palma's *tradición* is not due only to his desire to bring his work closer to the people. Orality, as is known, is a common trait of all nineteenth-century writing, which is founded on the logocentric link between voice and authorial presence. The text's "authority" (in all senses of the term) was based on its supposed reproduction of the author's voice through writing. In many nineteenth-century texts, orality is a way of evoking the figure of the author, who, like a supreme dictator or guide, joins the elements of his text in a totality that aspires to be harmonious. Palma was not immune to this literary myth so common in his age; it is implicit in the style of his *Tradiciones* and appears explicitly in many passages of his correspondence.[4] Bearing this in mind, it is easy to see that the intense orality of Palma's *tradición* is due precisely to its lack of generic definition. Few nineteenth-century literary genres require the textual "presence" of their author as much as the *tradición*. Because of its inherent instability and generic vagueness, the *tradición* needs the continuous support of its creator, its demiurge, in order to function. Without the figure of the author, which is made present in the text not only through "voice" but also by means of autobiographical allusions, the *tradición* would dissolve into a mass of unconnected facts, thus revealing its underlying textual framework. Nevertheless, unlike the powerful authorial presence seen in most other nineteenth-century narratives (from Balzac and Stendhal to Galdós, Flaubert, and Zola), the authorial "voice" in the *Tradiciones* tends to question and subvert its own authority by revealing the textual mechanisms that underlie the *tradición* and (as Escobar rightly notes) by the *"carácter non finito,"* the unfinished nature, of the text (p. 139). There is a tantalizing play between orality and textuality that intensifies the slippery, undefinable nature of the text, and suggests that Palma's *tradición* contains, from the very beginning, its own self-criticism.

Clearly, then, the *Tradiciones'* orality cannot be seen, as Escobar suggests, as their most typical and defining trait; this would not merely imply falling into the trap of the Romantic literary ideology; it would imply ignoring their patently textual nature. Palma was not the mere "secretary" of the multitudes, the romantic *vates* who directly transcribed the "voice" of the people into a literary style. To produce the effect of orality in his writings, he made use of various textual mediations, the most important of which, in my view, is that of journalism. I do not intend to argue here that journalism is the "key" to the generic specificity of the *Tradiciones*. As I stated earlier, Palma's *Tradiciones* do not encourage such simple solutions. Instead, I am proposing that Palma strategically used certain elements of the journalistic writing of his period in order to stress the critical (as well as populist) side of his work.

Palma's contacts with journalism are well documented, and it is immediately evident that he was most closely associated with the satiric and humoristic sort. As an adolescent, Palma edited the satirical broadside *El Diablo* (1848) and collaborated in *El Burro* (1852) and *La Zamacueca Política* (1859; Miró, p. 140). In 1867, he directed the newspaper *La Campana*, whose rhymed motto was: "Periódico nacional y caliente, / que ni verdades calla, ni mentiras consiente" ("National newspaper that's red-hot, / which neither shuts up the truth nor permits lies"), and in 1877 he founded *La Broma*, which announced itself as "Periódico satírico y mordiente . . . / terror y espanto de la mala gente" ("A newspaper satiric and biting . . . / that terror into the bad guys is striking"; Angélica Palma, pp. 77–8). In 1851, Palma had been a chronicler and proofreader in *El Correo de*

Lima. The first versions of some of his *Tradiciones* were published from 1859 to 1861 in *El Liberal, El Diario, La República*, and *La Revista de Lima* (Oviedo, p. xiii). During his exile in Chile (1860–3), Palma also published in the journals *Revista del Pacífico* and *Revista de Sud América* (Oviedo, p. xiv). Among the various foreign newspapers on which he collaborated were Buenos Aires' *La Prensa*, New York's Spanish-language paper *Las Novedades*, and Panama City's *La Estrella de Panamá* (all during the 1880s; Angélica Palma, pp. 85–6). Palma also collaborated on several occasions with the venerable Lima daily *El Comercio* (Miró, p. 141).

What elements of journalism subsist in the *Tradiciones peruanas*? And which of these contribute most visibly to intensify the *Tradiciones*' critical nature? We might begin by pointing out the importance of journalism as one of the sources for and as a thematic leitmotif in the *Tradiciones*. Although it is true that his sources are mainly historical (chronicles, *relaciones*, memoirs, annals, and the like) and folkloric (old wives' tales, jokes, folktales, aphorisms), Palma also makes use of information that appears in Colonial as well as contemporary Peruvian newspapers and journals. Among the Colonial newspapers mentioned in his writings are the *Gaceta de Lima* (1744), the *Diario de Lima* (1790), the *Diario Erudito* (1790), and *El Mercurio Peruano* (1791). These scattered allusions to the earliest Peruvian newspapers, along with his comments in the *Tradiciones* titled "Los plañideros del siglo pasado" and "El 'Aviso,'" show the good firsthand knowledge Palma had of the history of journalism in Peru.[5]

Allusions to contemporary newspapers are more frequent in those *Tradiciones* set in "Constitutional Peru" (according to the chronological reordering proposed by Edith Palma). Some *tradiciones* dealing with this period, such as "Un fanático," "Tirar la banda por el balcón," "Respuesta a una rectificación," and "'Callao' y 'chalaco,'" are based on newspaper articles or were motivated by them, while others, such as "Entre Garibaldi . . . y yo," present autobiographical information about Palma's participation in Lima's journalism.[6] At times, Palma bases his narrative on articles by other *tradicionistas* and essayists on manners, such as "Perpetuo Antañón" and Modesto de la Fuente ("Fray Gerundio"; Palma, pp. 233, 602–3).

But, journalistic sources aside, it is clear that Palma handled (or read) his historical and folkloric sources *as if they were* journalism. This can be seen in the curious temporal effect the *Tradiciones* have upon their historical sources: Although the predominant verb tenses used in the *Tradiciones peruanas* are, as one might expect, the preterite and the imperfect, in these texts Palma narrates and comments on events in the more or less remote past as if they were recent occurrences. He frequently suggests parallelisms and/or contrasts between previous ages and his own, zigzagging between past and present in a way that tends to contaminate the past with the forms of the present. The following passage from "Motín de limeñas" is a good example. In this *tradición*, Palma refers to the protests that arose in Lima in 1601 against King Phillip II's sumptuary edict forbidding certain elements of women's clothing, including a certain type of shoe:

> The deuce with these limeñas, who were (and still are) devilishly obsessed with wearing pretty little shoes, because, as my grandmother used to say, *the kettle heats from the bottom up!* How dare the king come out with pragmatic sanctions against satin shoes and booties! . . . What a dirty card-deck king!
>
> Let's see if there's any father or husband nowadays who dares to legislate in his home against high heels à la Louis XV! I challenge the bravest man to do it.
>
> > *With a silken stocking*
> > *And a nice little shoe,*
> > *Though you might be a saint,*
> > *Limeñas will make you sin too.*
> > (p. 235; italics in original)

Save in rare cases, Palma does not attempt to preserve and evoke the strangeness and exoticism of Colonial life; instead, he tries to bring that time closer to his readers. This he does by means of rhetorical and stylistic devices that make the subject matter of his narration familiar to his readers and by paying particular attention to the most minute details of everyday life, to gossip and rumors, to the *petite histoire*, instead of to great political and military deeds. In interpreting his historiographic sources, Palma suppresses their monumental aspects and emphasizes their marginal, human side. It should be remembered, in any case, that not a few of Palma's historical sources consist of letters, legal documents, and other heterogeneous and non-historiographic texts in which the events of the Peruvian past appear "in the rough," untouched by the historian's attempt at synthesis, and with a quasi-journalistic immediacy. One could argue, using a well-known concept developed by Mikhail Bakhtin, that Palma "carnivalizes" Peruvian history, since he always tends to narrate it from a down-to-earth perspective, "from the waist down" (Bakhtin, pp. 368–436). Nevertheless, to state this about Palma still begs the question of exactly how he does it; in my view, it is by using the techniques and devices of journalism.

Let us examine those techniques in their relationship to the style and the plots of the *Tradiciones peruanas*. The style of the *Tradiciones* derives in large part from the satirical journalism of the first half of the nineteenth century. Although virtually all journalism written in the early nineteenth century had literary aspirations, satirical journalism was more deliberately so, since it frequently used the mold of narrative fiction, of poetry, or of a combination of both (this last is very common in Palma's *Tradiciones*). Furthermore, although satirical journalism took as its subject situations, people, and events from real life, its intention was less to inform than to chastise, and it therefore made use of a whole arsenal of rhetorical tropes, from parody and irony to allegory.

It might be argued that the term "satirical journalism" is imprecise, since it includes texts that could properly be classified as essays on manners. Nevertheless, although many essays on manners (such as those by the Spaniard Mariano José de Larra) had strong satirical elements, in general their purpose was to produce a broader sort of social criticism and analysis. The essayists on manners usually aspired to present a total image of their society by means of a tabulation of social or national *types*. Like guardsmen peering through the windows of a panopticon, these writers sought to capture a panoramic view of their society from which they could later derive generalizations and stereotypes about their own nations.[7] Moreover, temporality in the essay on manners is usually expressed as a contrast between the past and present states of society, with the essayist tending to privilege the past. Satirical journalists, on the other hand, although working within the same broad field of the observation of manners, write for more immediate and localized reasons. They are also moved by a very journalistic concern with novelty. Whereas essayists on manners generally deal with the almost-unchanging patterns and details of everyday life, satirical journalists focus on "news" – on that which upsets or breaks the daily routine. The satirist's gaze, unlike the essayist's, fixes on the present in order to move toward the future. Also, whereas the essayist on manners is content with producing a "physiognomy" of society in a given epoch, the satirical journalist seeks to correct the evils that arise daily in society.[8] In fact, as a literary device, satire always requires almost journalistic speed and immediacy. Few literary genres are as fragile as satire, which quickly loses its vigor when the people or circumstances that motivate it are gone.[9] Satirical journalism, then, is doubly dependent on presentness and immediacy, since it must not only communicate news, but also comment on it quickly before it loses its relevance.

Traces of satirical journalism's corrective mordacity can still be observed in the style of Palma's *Tradiciones,* along with a tendency to read historical texts as if they dealt with contemporary events of Palma's day. What Palma does is to *translate* historical discourse into the discourse of satirical journalism. This tends to weaken the satirical content of his texts, since the target of the satire lies in the past, but it also tends to make the historical text more contemporary by bringing it closer to his readers' epoch and forcing them to read history satirically, as if it dealt with questionable present-day occurrences.

The presence of a satirical style in the *Tradiciones* also induces the reader to look for an allegorical interpretation that would connect them to the present and thus make the satire more effective. For example, in "La endemoniada," when Palma states that Ursulita, the possessed woman, was "a house inhabited by malignant spirits, more unwilling to change their dwelling-place than a cabinet minister to resign from his post" (p. 163), he is obviously inviting readers to seek the target of his satire in a time and place other than the seventeenth century. Raúl Porras Barrenechea correctly observes that the criticism of authority (be it of the king, the viceroy, or a *paterfamilias*) visible in the *Tradiciones peruanas,*

has a certain air of opposition journalism. . . .
. . . Without realizing it, the *tradicionalista* forgets his duties as a historian in order to chastise the political parties and leaders of his own time. His language is the first to betray him. It is the political

satirist who speaks when Palma ironically refers to bullets as "democracy pills," or when he says that the teacher in one of his tales "granted a general amnesty" to his beleaguered students. . . . There are many such allusions in the *Tradiciones*. With the slightest pretext, the chronicler foresakes the past for the present that never ceased to preoccupy him. (in Flores, *Orígenes del cuento hispanoamericano*, pp. 66–7)

It is instructive to compare a fragment of nineteenth-century satirical journalism with a passage from one of Palma's texts. A good example of the former is found in the article "Porquerías y adefesios" ("Filth and Ugliness") from *Museo de limeñadas* (1853) by Ramón Rojas y Cañas (who is considered Palma's precursor):

There's no need to be alarmed, gentle limeñas; nor should you begin, with dainty gestures of repugnance, to turn up your nose with loathing and annoyance when you read the patronymic name of this article.

You can read it with confidence, because although its title is like that, half dirty, its contents are not.

This will therefore be a hypocritical article, one that says different things from what it promises in its title. – All right! So at least it has some good quality, even though it is simply that of resembling human beings: – Yes, those men who show themselves on the vespers of la Merced or Santo Domingo, kneeling and crossing themselves, hitting their own chests with terrible blows as a sign of contrition, giving devout little kisses to the floor, and as soon as they leave the church, after handing the steward of the celebration the alms-box with more than half the oblation collected, run off to the little portal of San Agustín to the . . . daguerreotype machines, to take seemly pictures of their cartoonish figures.

Although the title of this article bears the words *filth* and *ugliness*, it is not my intention to allude to filthy or fetid things.

May God punish me if I am ever so foolish as to make people read in print some dirty thing . . . such as *dead dog . . . rotten mule*, on the cover of our own journal, nor anything that can be interpreted by malicious people as an allusion to cleanliness.

But enough preludes, and let's get to the point; or, in a more typical saying, "menos pañitos y más chocolate," as every born and bred limeño says. (pp. 268–9; italics in original)

Let us compare this with a fragment of the *tradición* "Zurróncurrichi" from the Fifth Series of the *Tradiciones peruanas* (1883):

Surely, my dear reader, you must often have heard people say: *Puneña, zurrón-currichi*, referring to the women of San Carlos de Puno, an appellation that, frankly, is one of the worst that can be made to the women born there, because it means calling them witches, and they would be fully justified in drinking the last drop of blood of the scoundrel who so rascally insults them.

I wouldn't say that the thing has much basis in fact; but it must have some, since that city is on the slopes of the *Laycacota,* which in Cervantes' Spanish means something like *witches' lair.*

Nevertheless, looking through my *Annals of the Inquisition of Lima,* a sort of book I wrote and published I don't remember how nor when, I do not find that the Holy Office ever punished a single witch from Puno, even though the list I made of them, with all their abilities and circumstances, is pretty long and detailed.

But if tradition states that there were witches in Puno, this doesn't mean (and here I hope to earn the esteem of the girls who currently break bread in Puno) that there are any today, and if there are, I'll be darned if they use other charms than those God put in their doe's eyes and their coral-colored little mouths.

After this introduction I think I can, without fear of being scratched, narrate the story or happening. (p. 444; italics in original)

I have deliberately chosen two passages that have much in common: Both are the introduction to their respective articles, both are addressed to a feminine readership, and in both the point of departure is a commentary or gloss of some popular phrase or expression. Another important similarity that goes beyond thematic considerations has to do with the *tone* of the two passages, which is typical of satirical journalism. Informal and bantering, it relies on diminutives and colloquialisms, and frequently verges on caricature. Nevertheless, there are significant differences in how the two passages approach their subject. Rojas y Cañas' is a true satire, directed against the idiomatic expressions used by the men and women of Lima in those days. In writing this, he ran the risk of alienating his readers – which explains the whimsical tone of his text. In contrast, in Palma's text what we see is merely the form or the rhetorical framework of satire (the humorous tone, use of diminutives, caricature) and, although the narrator is also careful not to adopt a polemic posture with regard to his readers, his target is not as clear.

The basic difference between these texts lies in their attitude toward time and history: Rojas y Cañas speaks about the present; Palma's text, although it may be interpreted in terms of the present, deals manifestly with past events. As was said earlier, Palma pours his historical materials in the mold of satirical journalism, thus stripping them of their usual seriousness, "carnivalizing" them and dissolving history into a series of unconnected episodes of doubtful value as knowledge. By transposing historical materials into a quasi-literary genre such as satirical journalism, Palma demonstrates the considerable dependence of historical discourse on rhetorical strategies and literary devices to produce a truth-effect, and implicitly questions the nineteenth-century tendency to link history with truth. His satire of the present then becomes oblique and cautious, while paradoxically acquiring a more profoundly critical dimension, since it attacks not only the people and circumstances of Palma's time and place, but also historical discourse (with its claims of absolute truthfulness) and the conservative ideology that used such a discourse to support itself. In sum, Palma's satirical style leads him toward a moderate and politically liberal version of the pessimistic concept of history discerned in Burckhardt by Hayden White:

> The story that Burckhardt told of the past was always the story of a "fall" from high achievement to bondage. All that is left for the historian to consider, after this "fall" occurs, is the historical artifact, conceived as "fragments" and "ruins," the pathos of which derives from the cry contained within them for the "remembrance of things past." This remembrance of things past is the sole obligation of the historian. He is required not to impose upon the fragments fables that might inspire to heroism in the present. He is not permitted to "dramatize" them in such a way as to induce faith in the healing capacities of cooperative social action. And he is specifically enjoined from seeking the general laws of historical, and cosmic, process which might give to living generations a confidence in their own capacities to revive their flagging powers and to press on to the struggle for a proper humanity.[10]

If the style of satirical journalism contributes much to the critical nature of the *Tradiciones peruanas,* the stories Palma chooses to retell contribute no less. In them we find traces of another modality or subgenre of journalism, the *fait-divers* (the French term gives a better idea of what it is than the names given to it in English: "filler," or "human-interest story.") The *fait-divers,* as Roland Barthes notes, cannot be placed in any of the broad categories into which news is divided in modern journalism (politics, economy, war, entertainment, science, etc.; *Critical Essays,* p. 185). It usually deals with events that are trivial and "strange," and sometimes either humorous, tragic, or absurd: *An Englishman enlists in the Foreign Legion: to avoid spending Christmas with his mother-in-law; Old man strangled by the cord of his hearing aid;* and *Iceland fishermen net a cow* are some of the examples quoted by Barthes (*Critical Essays*, p. 190). The *fait-divers*, which has been a clearly defined category of news since the early nineteenth century (González, *La crónica modernista hispanoamericana*, p. 73), is distinguished from other types because it lacks their episodic quality. Unlike political, military, or judicial news, whose structure, according to Barthes, is similar to a novel's, the *fait-divers* does not form a part of a longer narrative that is unfolded in a period of several days or which needs to be evaluated in a broader context (*Critical Essays*, p. 186). Instead, it possesses an immanence, a narrative self-sufficiency, analogous to that of the short story:

> the *fait-divers* . . . is total news, or more precisely, immanent; it contains all its knowledge in itself; no need to know anything about the world in order to consume a *fait-divers;* it refers formally to nothing but itself; . . . on the level of reading, everything is given within the *fait-divers;* its circumstances, its causes, its past, its outcome; without duration and without context, it constitutes an immediate, total being which refers, formally at least, to nothing implicit; in this it is related to the short story and the tale, and no longer to the novel. It is its immanence which defines the *fait-divers*. (*Critical Essays*, p. 186)

It is easy to see that, in terms of content (leaving aside their historical nature) as well as structure, the vast majority of the *Tradiciones peruanas* could be placed under the rubric of the *fait-divers*. For example, the *Tradiciones* share with the *fait-divers* the same narrative immanence indicated by Barthes: Palma's texts contain in themselves virtually all the information needed for their interpretation. This is clearly evident in the structure of the *Tradiciones*. Most begin with an introduction in which facts from Palma's life are related, we are given an explanation of why the text was written, or the sociohistoric context is explained, as in "Una moza de rompe y raja," in which Palma begins by saying: "Without the historico-economic information I am going to present here, which is very relevant to today's banking crisis [note the satiric and journalistic allusion to a contemporary event], it might be difficult for my readers to understand this *tradición*" (p. 968). This introduction is usually followed by an anecdote that frequently has a short-story-like structure, but is interrupted by an *"obligado parrafillo histórico"* ("obligatory little historical paragraph," as Palma refers to it more than once) that, aside from creating suspense in the story, provides additional information to aid our understanding of the narrative.

It could be argued that the *Tradiciones,* unlike the *fait-divers* as defined by Barthes, *do* require a context, and are therefore not "immanent" at all. Their historical content indeed sets them apart in a strict sense but, just like satirical journalism, the *Tradiciones* evoke the form of the *fait-divers,* although with a different meaning. I do not mean to suggest, in any event, that the *Tradiciones* are reducible to the model of the *fait-divers;* instead, I wish to point out how Palma uses certain aspects of this journalistic subgenre for his own textual aims.

As Barthes explains, the *fait-divers* is structured along either of two explanatory strategies: causality or coincidence. Causality in the *fait-divers,* however, is always aberrant, problematic:

the slight volume of a cause in no way diminishes the scope of its effect; a little equals a lot; and thereby this "deranged" causality can be everywhere: it is not constituted by a quantitatively accumulated force, but rather by a mobile energy, active in very small doses. (*Critical Essays,* p. 190)

Coincidence in the *fait-divers,* in contrast, is never free from the possibility of establishing a causal relationship:

When the safecrackers open the blowtorch manufacturer's safe with a blowtorch, this notation can ultimately belong only to the category of signs, for the meaning (if not its content, at least its idea) inevitably derives from the conjunction of two oppositions: antithesis or paradox, all contrariety belongs to a deliberately constructed world: a god prowls behind the *fait-divers.* (p. 194)

Finally, Barthes notes that the *fait-divers* exists in an ambiguous area in which causality and chance, literature and journalism, mingle and intermix, in which events are turned into *signs* whose meaning is always uncertain (p. 194).

It is in their narrative plots that the *Tradiciones* most resemble the *fait-divers,* with the most common sort of story being one that narrates unusual events, inexplicable coincidences, and/or bizarre crimes. The stories in the *Tradiciones* also explore the problematic relationship between causality and chance, and it is obvious that they thrive on the same fundamental ambiguity as the *fait-divers*. Like the latter, the *Tradiciones* can be divided into two kinds: those that explore a causal relation (the origin or cause of a certain proverb or popular expression, for example), and those that expose a coincidence, such as when, in "Los pasquines del bachiller 'Pajalarga,'" we are told:

> *Pajalarga* reached Panama: but in crossing the Chagres river, he fell from his mule and . . . and . . . (guess what!) and . . . he was eaten by an alligator.
> Don't take my word for it, nor say that I've made up this way of finishing off the protagonist of the story. That is how Calancha tells it, and he adds this picturesque phrase: *and the punishment was proportional to the crime, since he lived backbiting and he died bitten.* (p. 155; elisions and italics in original)

The *Tradiciones* also show the same uncertain mixture of causality and coincidence, of truthful information and literary re-telling, seen in the *fait-divers*. Among the many instances of this is the *tradición* "El alcalde de Paucarcolla (De cómo el diablo, cansado de gobernar en los infiernos, vino a ser alcalde en el Perú)." This text narrates various incidents that occurred in the seventeenth century in the town of Paucarcolla, on the shores of Lake Titicaca. The town's mayor was an Andalusian named Don Angel Malo (which is one of the euphemisms for the Devil in Spanish, roughly the same as "Fallen Angel"). In spite of the fact that Don Angel Malo was, to all accounts, an exemplary mayor who banished vagrants and scoundrels from his town, pressured bachelors into marrying, and fomented religious devotion, the unfortunate combination of his first and last names, along with certain details of his clothing (such as his "red cape bordered with chinchilla"), plus the fact that he never married nor ever went into any church, made the citizens suspicious. These suspicions were apparently confirmed when the mayor lent his mule to a friar who was taking a message to Lima, and the friar's muleback trip took a prodigiously short time. The friar then contacted the Inquisition and accused the mayor of being a sorcerer. When the agents of the Holy Office tried to arrest the mayor, he fled along the shores of Lake Titicaca and was never seen again. The narrator then remarks: "It is likely that Don Angel must have wandered, like a fugitive, hither and yon, until he reached Tucumán or Buenos Aires, or he must have taken refuge in Brazil or Paraguay, because nobody in Puno ever had news from him again. This is my belief, which is as good as any other. Or so it seems to me" (p. 273). However, he immediately adds: "But the people of Paucarcolla, whose reasons are well-founded, swear and affirm that the red-caped individual who came out of the lake and had himself named mayor was the Devil himself, and that he sank with his cape in the lake when, his deceit uncovered, he was in danger of having ashes put on his brow by the Inquisition" (p. 273). The narrator decides to retain the two interpretations of the event, thus keeping the tale suspended in a gray zone in which it is difficult to separate causality from coincidence: Did Don Angel Malo not attend church because he was a Moorish convert (p. 271), or because he was the very Devil? What was the reason for his apparent chastity? Did the friar arrive in Lima in twenty days because the mule really was quick, or because it was bewitched? Was it simply a coincidence that the mayor's name was Angel Malo? The bantering tone in which the *tradición* is narrated, far from tipping the scales to the side of incredulity, actually strengthens the ambiguity of the *fait-divers*, because we cannot tell when the narrator is joking and when he is serious.

Furthermore, the evocation we see in this text of the Devil as a tutelary figure of the *Tradiciones* is highly significant. It is worth quoting some passages from the introduction to "El alcalde de Paucarcolla":

One must agree that what they call civilization, enlightenment, and progress in this century has done us a disservice by suppressing the Devil. In Colonial times, when His Grace went around, feeling more self-important than Cardinal Camarlengo, and chatting with the progeny of Adam, there was barely a case of suicide or incestuous love every fifty years or so. Out of fear and respect for the hot coals and molten lead, sinners agonized in uncertainty before committing crimes that today are common occurrences. Today the Devil has nothing to do, for good or ill, with us miserable mortals; the Devil has already gone out of fashion, and not even the friars mention him in the pulpit; the Devil is dead and buried.

If, by one of God's miracles, I am again elected to Congress, I shall have to present a new law to resuscitate the Devil and return him to the full performance of his ancient duties. We need the Devil; give him back to us. When the Devil lived and there was a Hell, there was less vice and roguery in our land.

In the name of *pyrotechnic* history and *phosphorescent* literature, I protest the suppression of the Evil One. To eliminate the Devil is to kill tradition. (pp. 270–1; italics in original)

As in the *fait-divers*, in the *tradición* "a god prowls behind." Like the *fait-divers*, the *Tradiciones* postulate the existence of a demiurge whose intervention turns coincidence into causality and brings order to the narrative. Palma's statement, "To eliminate the Devil is to kill tradition" ("*Eliminar el diablo es matar la tradición*"), though equivocal (in which sense does he use the term "*tradición*"?), suggests the importance he gives to a certain "narrative theology" that postulates the need for a causal principle, a demiurge or author, for the literary work.

The ambivalent Romantic figure of the Devil, besides being a prototype of rebelliousness and marginality, is a species of messenger or bridge between world and otherworld, causality and coincidence, literature and history, and it clearly plays a key role in the *Tradiciones peruanas*.[11] The demon appears or is evoked in many of the *Tradiciones,* functioning in them not only as the author's mask or alter ego – which, added to the autobiographical references and the orality, serves to strengthen Palma's "authority" over his text – but also as another sign of their journalistic connections. For, although he was a typical figure in Romantic literature, nineteenth-century journalism, particularly of the satirical kind, also made use of the Devil. Let us recall the title of one of the newspapers Palma directed in his youth: *El Diablo.*

As Margarita Ucelay Da Cal has shown, satiric journalism and the essay on manners have a common origin: the picaresque satire of Francisco de Quevedo and Vélez de Guevara in the seventeenth century, whose central figure was the "diablo cojuelo" (pp. 49–52, 85–93). By using the figure of the Devil as their alter ego, nineteenth-century authors underlined the secondary, critical origin of their authority; the demon – attempted usurper of the Father's place, "bastard" emanation of the deity – appears as a figure that questions the principle of authority by divine right and the genealogical framework that supported the political and aesthetic conservatism of the age.[12] It could even be said that, up to a point, the character of the Devil appears in the *Tradiciones peruanas* as the incarnation of their spirit of negative criticism; it symbolizes the dissociative energy that presides over the radical ambiguity of the *Tradiciones* and questions the genealogical foundations of nineteenth-century historical discourse. Paradoxically, however, the Devil appears in Palma's texts as an eminently historical, earthly being whose participation in human events is more visible in some ages than in others ("In Colonial times, . . . His Grace went around . . . chatting with the progeny of Adam. . . . Today the Devil has nothing to do, for good or ill, with us miserable mortals"). Palma's demon also symbolizes the critical aspect of history, its subversive underside, which produces and reveals the parade of human vanity and wickedness. Following the *Tradiciones*' antigenealogical thrust, the figure of the Devil is evoked also – explicitly or implicitly – in those *Tradiciones* in which Palma uncovers scandals among the ancestors of people from Lima's high society: "Mujer y tigre," "Un señor de muchos pergaminos," "La emplazada," "Amor de madre," "Capricho de limeña," "El conde condenado," and many others.

When I say that these texts are antigenealogical and that their journalistic elements contribute to this characteristic, I am alluding, on the one hand, to the fact that Palma refuses to organize his presumably historical writings following the model of generational succession that was customary in the nineteenth century, not only in historiography but also in narrative fiction (as in the novels of Balzac, Galdós, and Zola). Collections of Palma's *Tradiciones* that attempt to organize them in a historical sequence (such as the one by Palma's own granddaughter, Edith), violate the intentions of their author, who could have ordered them thus himself, had he wished.[13] On the other hand, by stressing the rhetorical similarities between literature and history, Palma questions the validity of genealogy as a method of historical research in much the same way that Friedrich Nietzsche does in *The Genealogy of Morals* (1887) and in "The Use and Abuse of History" (in *Thoughts out of Season*, 1873–6).[14]

But one does not need to go so far to find evidence for the antigenealogical impulse in Palma. In many *Tradiciones*, he deals quite literally with genealogies, beginning his texts with a description of the coat of arms of his noble characters, and even prefacing one of them ("Una ceremonia de jueves santo") with a genealogical tree. Nevertheless, in general, when Palma al-

ludes to the ancestry of his characters it is not with the intent
of praising them or of building a narrative framework but rather to make fun of them and to ridicule the excessively neat
causal sequence posited by genealogical trees. In "Una ceremonia de jueves santo," for example, after describing in great
detail (and with abundant satirical commentary) the family tree
of one of the characters, the anecdote that follows is so trivial
that we soon realize that the genealogical tree is totally unneces-
sary as a causal explanation for the story. In most of the other
Tradiciones in which Palma alludes to coats of arms and genealogies, such as "Un señor de muchos pergaminos," "Un escudo de armas," and "Un litigio original," the sordid and ridic-
ulous tales we hear are in stark contrast with the solemnity of
the genealogical images. "Un escudo de armas," for instance,
deals precisely with the murky business of buying and selling
titles of nobility:

Among the endless Castillian titles of nobility that existed in Peru,
not even six, perhaps, were truly granted by the Crown as recognition
of merits or as a reward for important services. When the Royal Trea-
sury was empty of coins (and this happened most of the time), the
King exploited the Peruvians' innocence and, much as government
bonds are sold today, nobiliary parchments were marketed and sold in
Lima for as much as thirty or forty thousand *duros.* . . .
One could always find a king-at-arms who, for a few *duros* more or
less, would paint a very bushy and pretty genealogical tree filled with
royal parentages that would make any ordinary Joe the linear descendant of none other than King Solomon and one of his concubines, or
of the bedding of the Queen of Sheba with the Cid Campeador. . . .
To a heraldist, not even the honesty of the chaste Susannah is safe
from calumny and slander, for if a bumpkin insists (and pays for it),
they will make him by $a + b$ the descendant of one of the libidinous
elders. . . . Only the people of Buenos Aires had the good sense not to
waste money on such foolery. Although the records show that many
Bulls of the Holy Crusade were sold over there, none indicates that
there was any demand for titles of nobility. . . . In Buenos Aires,
nobody wanted a title, either bought or given. Over there, men were
satisfied to be lineal descendants of Adam and indirect descendants
of Noah. In Buenos Aires, everyone, man or woman, is genuine rab-
ble, and it is impossible to find anyone who, as happens among us, has
indigo blue in his blood instead of red ocher.
In Peru and Mexico, then, anyone was a noble who could pay his
nobility in good coin; and let's leave it there, or else the Devil may
tempt me to stir up the hornets' nest. (pp. 811–12)

In this passage, one can clearly see how Palma uses the style of satirical journalism to ridicule the Peruvian elite's aspirations of nobility, and how Palma's demon of causality again makes a fleeting appearance ("or else the Devil may tempt me to stir up the hornets' nest"). But beyond its satirical intention, one can also note the distrust with which Palma regarded any attempt at producing a coherent history based on a genealogical scheme. For Palma, as for Nietzsche, genealogies are fictions, a self-serving creation of certain people and/or social classes in order to justify their power a posteriori (Foucault, *Language, Counter-Memory, Practice,* pp. 155–9). And nineteenth-century historiography and the novel, because of their reliance on genealogy, are also the victims of Palma's mistrust. No wonder Palma always refused (aside from his *Anales de la Inquisición de Lima,* a rather callow and heterodox historical work) to write a solid and comprehensive history of Peru. In his "Prólogo" to the *Tradiciones cuzqueñas* by Clorinda Matto de Turner, he went so far as to state that "the History that disfigures, omits, or evaluates only acts that are convenient or in a convenient manner; the History that follows the spirit of a school or faction, does not deserve its name. The limits of the *tradición* are much less narrow and dangerous."[15] No wonder, also, that Palma never tried to reconstruct his only novel, *Los marañones,* a historical narrative about the life and crimes of the sixteenth-century conquistador Lope de Aguirre, after it was lost in a fire.[16]

By submitting the raw material of history to the acid test of satirical journalism and the *fait-divers,* Palma made a practical demonstration of the conventional nature of historical discourse and of its use as an instrument of power. Contrary to the impression they give before being read, the numerous and thick tomes of the *Tradiciones peruanas* contain neither a triumphant chronicle of the glories of Peruvian history nor a systematic analysis of Peruvian history and society (the phraseology of "Neither-Nor Criticism" is unavoidable here) in the manner of most nineteenth-century histories and novels from Michelet to Balzac. Instead, they contain a reduction and a mockery of those texts. It is altogether superfluous to ask (as many critics have done) what was Palma's real attitude toward Peruvian history – whether or not he felt nostalgic for Colonial times, for instance – what matters is the effect the *Tradiciones* have on our way of reading history. After Palma, it is impossible to read history (of Peru or anywhere else) without a profound distrust of its veracity. Probably surpassing his intentions, Palma's use of journalism and his antigenealogical attitude tend to negate the concept of "historical origin" itself: We have already noted how in the *Tradiciones peruanas* the past is frequently little more than a mask of the present, an indirect way to satirize current affairs. Palma's obsession with the past turns out to be, paradoxically, like philology for Nietzsche: an instrument to refute history, to break the bonds of a tragic past and of grotesque origins, in order to return to a ground zero, to a present moment from which to launch projects for renewal.[17]

5
Journalism and the self: the Modernist chronicles

Marinetti's main idea is that everything is in what is to come and almost nothing in the past. In an ancient painting he only sees "the artist's painful contortions in his effort to break the insurmountable barriers to his desire to fully express his dream." But have the moderns really achieved this? If we at least have to take one funeral bouquet every year to honor the "Gioconda," what shall we do with the contemporary painters of golf courses and automobiles? So: Onwards! But, to where? If Time and Space no longer exist, isn't it the same to go Forwards as Backwards?

Rubén Darío, "Marinetti y el futurismo" (1911),
in *Obras completas*, I, 616–23

The Spanish American Modernists were a group of writers whose relationship with journalism, along with their desire to define literature, to seek out its "essence," led them to a profoundly critical understanding of the nature of writing and of the literary craft. It is true that many other writers, in both Europe and North America, were also involved in journalism around the turn of the century, but what makes the Spanish American Modernists unique is the degree to which even the major figures in that movement, such as José Martí, Rubén Darío and José Enrique Rodó, depended on journalism not only to earn a living but also to publish their writings.[1] The Modernists also exhibited an abiding concern with literary theory that, in my view, derived as much from their experience as journalists as from their acquaintance with philology. But before commenting on the Modernists' experience with journalism and its effect on their work, I will review the nature of Spanish American Modernism.

In recent years, a sweeping reevaluation of the nature and significance of Spanish American Modernism has been taking place, inspired in part by the insights of Octavio Paz in *Children of the Mire* (1974), as well as by the very suggestive evocations of Modernism and the *fin de siècle* contained in works by major contemporary Spanish American novelists, from Carpentier's *Reasons of State* (1974) to García Márquez's recent *Love in the Time of Cholera* (1985).[2] A significant part of this reevaluation has been the virtual rediscovery of the Modernists' abundant prose, which had for so long been eclipsed by their brilliant poetry. As early as 1966, Iván A. Schulman had pointed out that the Modernists' aesthetic first took shape in their prose writings.[3] But only recently have critics begun to pay serious attention to the Modernist contribution to the novel, the essay, the short story, and to a peculiar, middle-of-the-road genre that the Modernists practiced with particular devotion: the *crónica* or journalistic chronicle.

This genre consisted of brief articles on virtually any subject, written in a self-consciously literary style, that were meant to be entertaining as well as informative. In fact, however, the Modernists made much more of the chronicles than what they were originally intended to. The chronicles became literary laboratories for the Modernists, places where they tried out new styles and ideas and made these known to other writers. In many instances, chronicles account for more than two-thirds of an author's published writings, as can be seen in the *obras completas* of such major Modernists as Martí, Nájera, Darío, Nervo, and Gómez Carrillo.

It is only when we take into account the vast amount of prose writings of the Modernists – and especially the *crónicas* – that we can begin to understand the seminal importance of Spanish American Modernism to the subsequent history of Spanish American literature. Modernism was more than just the Spanish American version of French Symbolism; it was, to use Octavio Paz's well-known phrase, a "literature of foundation." It was an all-encompassing revolution in Spanish American literary and intellectual life without which the current achievements of Spanish American narrative would have been impossible. What the Modernists effected was, in fact, a "textual modernization" of Spanish American literature by incorporating philology ("la *science exacte* des choses de l'esprit," as Ernest Renan defined it), literary criticism, into their writing (Renan, p. 143; see also

González, *La crónica* . . ., pp. 5–59). Philology, as systematized by Renan, Taine, and others with its encyclopedic cosmopolitanism, its vision of cultural renewal, its interest in religion, and above all its notion of language as an object, a thing endowed with a concreteness and history of its own, was one of the Modernists' chief models for their literary endeavor. Their knowledge of philology linked the Modernists with the most advanced and radical thinking about language and literature that Europe had produced so far. Furthermore, since philology aspired in the end to absorb all the other scientific disciplines as well as the arts (according to the project outlined by Renan), their link with it gave the Modernists the possibility of addressing nonliterary issues as well. In this respect, the influence of philology on Modernism joins with that of another modern institution that gradually and successfully contested philology's claims to authority and relevance: journalism.

Like philology, journalism, in its daily activity, makes use of texts, and it also aspires to an empirical understanding of the world. But there are significant differences between these forms of discourse: Philology regards texts as objects of knowledge, whereas journalism considers them merchandise; philology aspires to produce, from textual analysis, a totalizing synthesis, whereas journalism seeks to capture the instant, the fleeting moment, in all its empirical detail, without attempting a synthesis. In addition, journalism undermines the idea of the "author" – so vital to nineteenth-century literature and philology – because what matters most in journalism is information itself and not the individual who transmits it. Most of the Modernists, whose literary ideology was strongly influenced by philology, had to submit, in their daily lives, to journalistic work. They had to satisfy the demands of an eminently modern, eminently prosaic institution that profoundly questioned the transcendental values held by both literature and philology in the nineteenth century.

Spanish American Modernism was thus founded in the midst of a complex interplay between literature, philology, and journalism: These three textual institutions mark the frontiers of Modernism, in poetry as well as in prose.[4] Very schematically, we can say that Modernism adopted from philology its archaeological notion of language, its vision of words as artifacts.

From European literature (seen as an institution) Modernism took its subversion of philology, which European literature performed by regarding words not as objects of knowledge (as the philologists did) but as objects of pleasure, as "collectibles," or knickknacks upon a shelf. Finally, from journalism Modernism derived criteria of textual economy (brevity, superficiality) that, along with a sense of novelty, helped reach out to a broad readership. As can be seen in the chronicles, however, although the Modernists learned much from journalism, they were also deeply troubled by it. They were perturbed by the power journalism as an institution had over their daily lives and by the theoretical implications of journalism for literature as it was understood and practiced during the nineteenth century.

In 1893, the Cuban Modernist poet Julián del Casal included a scathing denunciation of what he saw as the evils of journalism in an essay devoted to the work of his friend, the journalist Bonifacio Byrne. It is worth quoting in full:

Journalism, as it is understood today among us, is the most nefarious institution for those who, not knowing how to place their pen in the service of petty causes, or disdaining the ephemeral applause of the crowds, are possessed by the love of Art. But of art for art's sake, not of that art that predominates in our society, that repugnant mass of local excrement which, like rotting food on golden dishes, is served up daily by the press to its readers. The first thing that is done to the journalist when he takes his post in the newspaper office is to deprive him of one of the writer's indispensable attributes: his own personality. . . . Thus the journalist, from the moment he begins his work, has to suffer through immense avatars according to the demands of his newspaper, turning into a republican if he is a monarchist, into a freethinker if he is a Catholic, or into an anarchist if he is a conservative. I will not mention here the thousand menial chores of journalism, the only ones to which young men of letters can aspire, because it would take me too long to enumerate them. Suffice it to say that some, such as those having to do with the gossip columns, are not only stupefying but also degrading. Journalism can be, in spite of its intrinsic hatred of literature, the benefactor that puts money in our pockets, bread on our table, and wine in our cup, but, alas, it will never be the tutelary deity that encircles our brow with a crown of laurel leaves. I know that it is more worthwhile, as Zola says, to scribble in a newsroom than to daydream in a garret. That may be true in magnificent France, where the journalist must be a man of letters, but not in unfortunate Cuba, where the journalist is, with few exceptions, the opposite of his Parisian colleague. (p. 272)

Casal's views are, in many ways, an extreme formulation of complaints that had been uttered much earlier by another of the early Modernists, the Mexican Manuel Gutiérrez Nájera. It was Nájera who, around 1880, inspired by the frivolous and gossipy *chroniques* published by French dailies such as *Le Figaro* and *La Chronique Parisienne,* imported the genre of the chronicle from France into Spanish America.[5] In an 1883 article titled, with evident irony, "His Majesty, the Journalist," Nájera observes that the journalist must be the sort of person who,

like the gods of Walhalla, can be chopped into a thousand pieces yet remain whole. Yesterday he was an economist, today he is a theologian, tomorrow he will be a Hebraist or a baker. He has to know how good bread is made and which are the laws of evolution. There is not one science he is not obliged to know, nor any art whose secrets he can ignore. The same pen with which last night he drafted a chronicle about the society ball or the theater will serve him today to write an article about railroads or banks, and all this without being able, because of the lack of time, to open a book or consult a dictionary.[6]

In a similar vein, the Cuban José Martí – who along with Nájera must be considered one of the inventors of the Modernist chronicle – had written, in his 1882 prologue to "El poema del Niágara" by Juan Antonio Pérez Bonalde,

There is now a sort of dismemberment of the human mind. Gone are the days of the high fences; this is the time of the broken fences. . . . People want to hear about everything. No sooner have thoughts germinated than they are loaded down with flowers and fruits, and jumping in the paper, and seeping, like a subtle powder, into every mind. Railroads tear down the jungle; newspapers tear down the human jungle. The sun shines through the cracks in the old trees. Everywhere one sees expansion, communication, flowering, contagion, dissemination. The newspaper deflowers grand ideas. Ideas no longer settle down in our mind, make it their home, nor do they live long in it. . . . We wake up with one problem; we go to bed with another. Images devour each other in our mind. There is not enough time for us to give shape to our thoughts. (*Obras Completas,* p. 235)

Recurring like a leitmotiv through these three quotations is a concern with journalism's effect on the writers' capacity to express themselves through their writing. The Modernists, like their Romantic predecessors, regarded literature as a vehicle for self-expression. The writer's self, embodied in the figure of the author and inscribed in the author's style, was not only the source of the text, but also its organizing, centering principle. Having an author was an essential characteristic of a "literary work" during the nineteenth century. It was not the only characteristic, of course; works could have an author and still not be considered "literary." But no true work of literature could be authorless, even if its author were "Anonymous" or, as in the case of the ballads and *romances* of which the Romantics were so fond, its author was the collective "voice of the people."

Journalism, as Martí, Nájera, and Casal noted, tended to erode the principle of authorship in two distinct ways. One was its emphasis on novelty, speed, and objectivity over familiarity, reflection, and analysis. What counts most in journalism, Martí remarks (almost anticipating television journalism), are images, not ideas; perception, not cognition. Journalism's authority does not emanate from the force of a writer's personality or even from the writer's "imagination" (that most prized of Romantic qualities), but from the impression of truthfulness it creates by communicating empirically verifiable events.

It is true that throughout the nineteenth century, journalistic style was still, by today's standards, highly "literary." As María Cruz Seoane has pointed out, oratory was the predominant model for journalistic writing until the 1880s (*Oratoria y periodismo*, pp. 12–18, 333–50). As we shall see, oratory survived in the Modernist chronicles, but even by the end of the century the character of journalism had changed radically. Until then, particularly in French- and Spanish-speaking countries, journalism had been closely allied with politics and what was then called "general enlightenment," that is, the dissemination of technical or scientific knowledge for the benefit of merchants and entrepreneurs (see Chapter 2). Where freedom of the press allowed it, there was "journalism of opinion," in which newspapers and magazines with different ideologies criticized the government or the various political parties. Where there was no freedom of the press, newspapers served to disseminate government decrees and the political ideology of the state. In either case, speech-making, with its emphasis on persuasion and rhetorical effects, was the model followed. But during the 1880s, spearheaded by newspapers in the United States and Great Britain, journalism became a mass phenomenon and a purely money-making enterprise; as sensationalist journalism flourished and the institution of the "reporter" came into existence, journalism began to divide into specializations: "journalism of opinion" was confined to what today are called "op-ed pages," and the front page was taken over by the short "news bulletin" transmitted from the scenes of events by the new technology of the telegraph (Stephens, pp. 202–11, 226–70; Cruz Seoane, *Historia del periodismo*, pp. 344–50). This naturally led to the abandonment of the oratorical model of journalistic style in favor of a more condensed "telegraphic style." Needless to say, the Modernists, although they were not fond of the pomposities of late nineteenth-century oratory, preferred to use it in their journalism because it at least gave them a chance at self-expression. The impersonal, reportorial "telegraphic style" was, for them, the very negation of style, and, therefore, of the author.

The second way in which journalism undermined the notion of the author was in its concept of texts as merchandise. The journalistic text was never written solely to satisfy aesthetic criteria; rather, it was tailored to what the editors of the newspaper or journal considered the public would pay to read about. Thus, the journalist had to be able to write in a wide range of styles on the most diverse subjects. Significantly, the term used in Spanish to refer to a member of the editorial staff of a newspaper is *redactor,* which means "writer" but in a sense is closer to the notion of "scribe" or "notary" than of "author." The term connotes a certain lack of originality, of spontaneity; it also stresses the *written* nature of the journalist's task, as opposed to the illusion of orality that was the stylistic ideal in nineteenth-century literature.

As we have seen, Nájera and Casal were particularly disturbed by this demotion of the author from a single coherent originator to a mere copyist or secretary. Moreover, as Nájera and Casal point out, journalism not only degrades the author, but it also "chops him to pieces." To be more precise, journalism forces the writer to assume different roles, or "avatars" in Casal's terms, never allowing him to speak with a single, coherent "voice" and frequently requiring him to use pseudonyms. Pseudonyms are, of course, a clear disavowal of authority. Nineteenth-century journalism frequently used them to hide the fact that the same writer was responsible for different sec-

tions of the newspaper. Pseudonyms did not protect a journalist (or his newspaper) from libel suits. However, by concealing
his identity from the general public (at least for a while), they
did protect him from being challenged to a duel, which in those
days was as common a predicament for journalists as to be sued
in court. Most Modernist chroniclers resisted the use of pseudonyms. One exception was Gutiérrez Nájera, who adopted this
practice wholeheartedly and, as we shall see, turned it to his
advantage.

Let us now turn our attention to precisely how three of the
most outstanding Modernist chroniclers (Martí, Nájera, and
Gómez Carrillo) reacted to the journalistic constraints we have
just examined. If, as mentioned earlier, Nájera can be credited
with introducing the French *chronique* into Spanish America,
José Martí was certainly the writer who gave this new genre a
higher intellectual content and an international diffusion.
From New York, where he lived for much of the latter part of
his life, Martí sent his chronicles to prominent Spanish American newspapers like *La Opinión Nacional* in Caracas and *La Nación* in Buenos Aires. These chronicles were also widely reprinted throughout the continent. Martí even contributed a
few articles, written in French and translated by someone else
into English, to the New York weekly *The Hour* and the daily *The
Sun,* owned by Charles Dana.[7] Martí, as is known, also founded
the newspaper *Patria* during the 1890s to further the cause of
Cuban independence.

Like most of the Modernists, Martí went into journalism not
only out of financial need but also because he was a writer, and
few other professions allowed him to earn money by doing
what he liked so much. He was particularly fortunate in being
able to deal with editors who knew of his stature as a man of
letters. For example, during his mature period as a journalist
(during the 1880s and 1890s) Martí never used pseudonyms
(he had used the pseudonym "Orestes" during his journalistic
apprenticeship in Mexico in the mid-1870s; see Vitier and García, pp. 195–199). He was also generally allowed considerable
stylistic freedom in his chronicles.

The chronicles of Martí fall into three general types: the
artistic and literary, the reportorial, and what we might call the
"domestic." This last type is represented by the series of texts

Martí wrote for the section titled "En Casa" ("At Home") of his newspaper *Patria* during the 1890s. In these chronicles, Martí recounted the modest social and political activities of the Cuban emigré community in New York, Tampa, and Key West. They are written in the lyrical yet familiar style one also finds in Martí's letters to his family and friends. In contrast, the artistic and literary chronicles, most of which date from the 1880s and were published in such diverse journals and dailies as *La Nación*, *El Partido Liberal* (Mexico), the *Revista Venezolana,* and *La Opinión Nacional,* have a lush descriptive style that has often been regarded as the epitome of the *"prosa artística"* ("artistic prose") of the Modernists. It is in the reportorial chronicles, however, that Martí uses the fullest range of stylistic and rhetorical devices. These texts were published during the 1880s and 1890s and collected in Martí's *Obras completas* under the headings "Escenas norteamericanas" ("North American Scenes") and "Escenas europeas" ("European Scenes"). I call these chronicles "reportorial" because they frequently deal with the sorts of events usually covered by reporters: political controversies, economic news, crime stories, disasters, etc. Nevertheless, Martí was not a "reporter" but a "foreign correspondent" and only rarely, such as at the inauguration of the Statue of Liberty in New York in 1886, did he chronicle an event that he had actually witnessed. His chronicles were in fact news summaries, gleaned mostly from North American and European newspapers (Vitier and García, p. 195). At a time when large international news agencies like Reuters were still relatively new, Martí operated as a sort of one-man news agency for many Spanish American publications.

The "Escenas norteamericanas" and "Escenas europeas" are the most abundant of the three types of chronicles Martí wrote, and may therefore be considered his most typical. Published weekly or fortnightly, these reportorial chronicles posed an enormous challenge to Martí's capacity as a writer, since he was required not only to enumerate and relate the week's events but also to comment on them within a coherent stylistic and ideological framework while keeping his discourse as impersonal as possible.

Martí performed this seemingly impossible task by avoiding the use of the first person as much as he could and assuming a

sort of "God's eye view" of events not unlike that of French
novelist Gustave Flaubert.[8] Unlike Flaubert, however, whose
highly ironic depiction of reality was intended to suggest that
reality was ultimately unintelligible (Culler, *Flaubert: The Uses of
Uncertainty,* pp. 185–207), Martí's chronicles presupposed an
underlying order to the often chaotic events being described.
The teeming masses of New York, the colonizers of the West,
the great statesmen and orators, the criminals, the intellectuals,
the civic celebrations, the public controversies, the disasters –
fires, earthquakes, railroad accidents – all the myriad characters and events of life in the United States and Europe that
parade through Martí's chronicles, are seen as part of a single,
coherent historical process. Even a natural catastrophe like the
Charleston earthquake of 1886 was interpreted by Martí, in
one of his best chronicles, as a providential event, a demonstration of mankind's capacity to move forward in spite of the de-
structive forces of nature.[9]

It is important to remember that Martí was one of the most
charismatic and powerful orators of his time and that part of
the effectiveness of his chronicles resides in their evocation of
the spoken word. The rhetorical tricks of oratory gave Martí's
chronicles an air of immediacy and coherence, with the disparate events narrated being "centered" and organized by the
author's disembodied voice. As the title *"Escenas norteamericanas"* suggests, events in Martí's chronicles are usually described as a sequence of tableaux or scenes, not unlike the
dioramas that were so popular in the Parisian arcades of the
mid-nineteenth century – in which each immobile scene was
brought to life by the voice and presence of an orator – or like a
museum, in which disparate exhibits are linked together by the
organizing discourse of the guide.[10] Martí sometimes inserted
himself in his chronicles as a sort of eyewitness, but even then
he used the third person, referring to himself in a curiously
disparaging fashion as "a certain outcast," "a stranger," or "an
insect."

Although avoiding the direct expression of his subjectivity,
Martí's chronicles are almost totally infused by his personal
ideas about history, society, and culture. Like his speeches, his
chronicles abound in aphorisms and maxims; for example:
"Man is nothing in himself, and what he is, is the product of his

people"; "Everything that exists is a symbol"; "Art is a form of respect." As an intellectual and a revolutionary leader, Martí realized that the chronicles could be used to educate his readers and to disseminate his political and social ideas. On various occasions, however, Martí's Spanish American editors censored his highly critical comments about the United States, and he became more oblique and suggestive in expressing his views (Quesada y Miranda, p. 105). Despite these obstacles, Martí was able to turn even the most informative of his chronicles into a highly personal text, written in a style that could not be mistaken for anyone else's. His success is attested by the grudging admiration evident in Domingo Faustino Sarmiento's comment to Paul Groussac in 1887: "There is nothing in the Spanish language like Martí's bellowing, and, aside from Victor Hugo, France has not produced a writer of such metallic resonance."[11]

Manuel Gutiérrez Nájera's response to the dissolution of the self in journalistic writing was, in many ways, the diametric opposite of Martí's. Whereas Martí sought to inscribe his self into his chronicles by means of a highly personal style and his aphorisms and allusions, Nájera's approach consisted of playing with the notion that the self was a fiction. As we have seen, this was one of journalism's most controversial legacies for nineteenth-century writers. Journalism's demotion of authority and authorship implies that, at least as far as writing is concerned, the self is an illusion, a phantom, an ephemeral effect produced by stylistic conventions and supported by the writer's signature at the foot of the text. Moreover, the journalistic requirements of factuality and impersonality reminded writers that, although they believe they are using language, language is also using *them*. In their unruly ambiguity, words imply things their writers never intended and bury every trace of the author's individuality in the semantic background noise produced by generations of language users. As the English Romantic William Wordsworth, in a rare moment of linguistic doubt, expressed it:

If words be not an incarnation of the thought but only a clothing for it, then they surely will prove an ill gift; such a one as those poisoned vestments, read of in the stories of superstitious times, which had the power to consume and to alienate from his right mind the victim who put them on. . . . Language, if it do not uphold and feed, and leave in quiet, like the power of gravitation or the air we breathe, is a counter-spirit, unremittingly and noiselessly at work to derange, to subvert, to lay waste, to vitiate, and to dissolve. (p. 154)

Wordsworth reminds us that if language can be molded, how-ever precariously, into a figment of selfhood, it can also corrode and dissolve the self, and, furthermore, it can become a locus of transformations where one fictional self is exchanged for another.

Nájera clearly understood this, although in the end he, like Wordsworth, was unwilling to renounce the idea of the self as the source of the literary text. As we have already seen, Nájera was aware of journalism's questioning of the Romantic notion of the text as a "work" – that is, as the unified, coherent expres-sion of an equally monolithic self (Barthes, *Image/Music/Text*, pp. 155–64). The chronicler had to be a person who, like a text, could be "chopped into a thousand pieces, yet remain whole." But how could this paradox be carried out? How could a single author cope with the demands for thematic and stylistic diver-sity imposed by journalism? Nájera's answer was the use of pseudonyms. Pseudonyms allowed Nájera to be inconsistent, or, to put it more generously, to be more flexible in terms of style in order to satisfy his editors. With pseudonyms, Nájera did not have to worry about maintaining a coherent literary persona throughout his writings, and he could afford to exper-iment and improvise. On the one hand, when asked to write frivolous social chronicles directed toward a mainly feminine readership, Nájera used the pseudonym "Puck" (an allusion to the mischievous elf in Shakespeare's *Midsummer Night's Dream*), and wrote in an appropriately gallant style. When, on the other hand, he was asked to write political satire, Nájera gave his series of articles the collective title of "Plato del día" ("Daily Special"), baptized himself "Recamier" (a famous chef of the period), and used a gently sarcastic, mocking style. Throughout his career, Nájera used more than twenty pseudonyms, includ-ing some that had already been used by other journalists. A partial list includes Fru-Fru, M. Can-Can, Fritz, Junius, Pom-ponet, Ignotus, Puck, Recamier, El Cura de Jalatlaco, Perico de los Palotes, and his favorite, El Duque Job.[12]

Nájera's use of pseudonyms can also be understood, of course, as a defensive and cautious gesture. If Martí himself, writing from the safety of New York, was often forced to moderate his views about the United States and to refrain from commenting on Spanish American politics in order to get his chronicles published in Argentina, Venezuela, or Mexico, Nájera and his colleagues in the newspapers of Porfirian Mexico had to be even more careful. As Boyd G. Carter points out in the Introduction to *Escritos inéditos de sabor satírico* (1972),

> In a period of such outright violations of press freedom and individual rights, it is not surprising that *El Duque Job* should put on the mask of humorism as a way of saving his job. By his use of ambiguities, double entendres, wordplay, puns, homonyms, parody, antiphrasis, and other such devices, he was able to precariously balance himself on the tightrope of polemical journalism, throwing his barbs at whomever he wanted, while avoiding persecution. He had of course to be circumspect, never exceeding the bounds of prudence, always giving an impression of ambiguous objectivity, and never forgetting to match his barbs against government officials with jokes against members of the opposition. Attacking the régime directly was unthinkable. Nájera could never forget that at home were his wife Cecilia, his firstborn daughter with the same name, and after 1894, his second daughter, Margarita, all depending for their sustenance on his skill with pen. (p. xii)

Pseudonyms were also an essential part of Nájera's strategy to achieve an uneasy coexistence between literature and journalism within the genre of the chronicle. Nájera's apparent denial of authority by his use of pseudonyms is paradoxically contradicted by his continuous insertion of artistically wrought fictional narratives into his journalistic texts. Many of his short stories (later collected in volumes like *Cuentos frágiles*, 1883) first appeared as chronicles or as parts of chronicles. The paradox disappears when we realize that Nájera was also using his pseudonyms as a cover for his fictions. The writer Manuel Gutiérrez Nájera might not have been allowed to "tell lies" in his articles, but El Duque Job's fictions could be justified as part of his already fictitious persona. By assuming fictional identities, Nájera cleared the way for the wholesale fictionalization of his chronicles.

Nájera's favorite symbol for the task of the chronicler was the Greek sea spirit Proteus, who could change his shape at will and foresee the future (*Larousse Encyclopedia of Mythology*, p. 151; Proteus later reappears in the essays of José Enrique Rodó). As

A. Bartlett Giamatti has pointed out, during the Renaissance the figure of Proteus had been a symbol of the *uomo universale*, the genius who resolves multiplicity into unity. This interpretation of the myth lasted throughout the nineteenth century, when Proteus was seen as "a figure for the writer's plenitude and grasp of all experience" (p. 448). Like the Renaissance humanists and the other nineteenth-century authors who evoked the sea-god as their emblem, Nájera preferred to downplay the existence of another, negative side of the Proteus myth that could also be seen as symbolic of journalism: An earlier tradition had regarded Proteus as an evil wizard, a sorcerer, and a figure of the chaos inherent in the natural world (Giamatti, pp. 438, 455, and passim). This Proteus was not a symbol of plenitude but of fragmentation, confusion, and defeat.

Nájera's awareness of this darker side of journalism is evidenced in the constant strain of melancholy that runs throughout his work. It can also be seen in the obituary he wrote on the death of his friend, the chronicler Alfredo Bablot, whose pseudonym was, in fact, "Proteus." There, Nájera exclaims: "And all that is lost now! . . . All that talent has burnt itself out like the fireworks display that shot such dazzling rockets into the air! It lies over there, in the newspaper archives that enclose thoughts like a coffin! It lies in his friends' memories, which also burn themselves out. . . .! The journalist writes for oblivion!" (*Obras. Crítica literaria*, I, p. 471).

Nájera's experience with pseudonyms brought him face to face with journalism's critical and corrosive effect on the literary ideology of the nineteenth century. Journalism's attempt to purge writing of all traces of selfhood in order to become a transparent medium of communication taught the Modernists that, in writing, the self counted for very little. That this linguistic transparency, this objectivity sought by journalism, is also an illusion would only be fully understood later by the Vanguardists; nevertheless, some Modernists also managed to glimpse this notion, as is evident in the writings of the last great Modernist chronicler, Guatemalan Enrique Gómez Carrillo.

Gómez Carrillo is remembered today only by specialists on Modernism, who generally regard him as a minor figure.[13] This is partly due to the fact that all of his work is in prose and consists mostly of chronicles. Unlike other Modernists, Gómez

Carrillo was first and foremost a journalist. That Gómez Carrillo, despite being a journalist and a prose writer, was considered one of the most prominent members of the Modernist pantheon in his time tells us much about how the Modernists viewed their own movement and about the critical prejudices that have distorted the understanding of Modernism by later generations.

The bulk of Gómez Carrillo's writing consists of travel chronicles. The accounts of the globe-trotting Guatemalan's journeys to many parts of the world, from Constantinople to Tokyo, were printed and reprinted in all the major turn-of-the-century Spanish and Spanish American newspapers. Because Gómez Carrillo lived in France for most of his adult life (he died in Nice in 1927), the rest of his chronicles deal with European social, cultural, and political events, and from a Spanish American point of view they can also be regarded as travel chronicles.

Because Gómez Carrillo was one of the last Modernists, it should come as no surprise that he was, along with José Enrique Rodó, one of the few explicit literary theoreticians of the movement, with essays such as "El arte de trabajar la prosa" ("The Art of Working with Prose") and his book *El modernismo* (1905). In one of his late chronicles, "La psicología del viaje" ("The Psychology of Travel," 1919), Gómez Carrillo reflects on the theory of travel writing. His comments show that he had already learned Nájera's lesson about the irrelevance of the self in journalism. He counsels the beginning travel writer to "avoid all psychology, since you know from Bourget that all psychological observations about foreign societies are pedantic inventions. Therefore, avoid also the study of personalities in the classical manner and all Romantic confessionalism. Don't talk about yourself! Don't be an egotist! What you do does not interest us" (p. 14). The travel writer must convey to his readers the pleasure of travel; that pleasure, Gómez Carrillo declares, consists in the gradual abandonment of the self: "Doesn't a French poet say that *partir c'est mourir un peu?* It is just this feeling of dying a little, this impression of passing abandon, that seduces us in traveling" (p. 13).

Gómez Carrillo's reflections on travel writing are set in the context of a profound skepticism toward travel as a means of acquiring knowledge, a skepticism that in turn undermines the very rationale for travel writing. Near the beginning of his essay, he paraphrases the French psychologist Paul Bourget's criticism of travel: "Why travel, asks the Parisian psychologist, when we shall never be able to know the souls of the people of other countries? Why go elsewhere in search of human documents, when we are not even able to decipher the documents of our own nation, our own family, our own self? The *know thyself* of the Greeks is a mere fantasy. We shall never know ourselves, just as we shall never know our fellow men" (p. 8). If traveling is useless as a means of understanding the self, reading and writing about it is even more so.

Gómez Carrillo finishes this highly self-critical chronicle by giving another reason for the futility of traveling and, indirectly, of the uselessness of travel writing: The new technologies of representation, particularly photography and film, are making physical travel nearly superfluous (pp. 17, 27–8). Moreover, from a purely representational point of view, photographs and movies are certainly far superior to the sensuously descriptive travel writing in which Gómez Carrillo specialized.[14] In the future, Gómez Carrillo implies, both literature and journalism, as well as the plastic arts, will have to invent, adopt, or adapt, new modes and new theories of representation in order to survive. Gómez Carrillo, however, was not fond of the avant-gardist experiments that were taking place in France all around him, and his work shows a nostalgia for the notions of selfhood, harmony, and order that is typically Modernist.

In Gómez Carrillo's somber meditations we find the opposite extreme from Martí's attitude toward the self at the dawn of the Modernist period. Martí, as we have seen, still believed in the self as the centering principle of writing and in the evocation of speech as an adequate means of representing reality: "*Decirlo es verlo*" ("To say it is to see it"), Martí declared in one of his chronicles. Nájera, for his part, tried to salvage the role of the self in writing by seeing it as a sort of mask, as a necessary fiction that allowed the writer to fight back against journalism's limitations of style and genre. Gómez Carrillo, who was a contemporary of the first European avant-garde movements, realized that the new technologies of photography and filmmaking would corrode still further not only the old notions of authority and authorship but also the empiricist epistemology on which journalism, along with all of nineteenth-century literature, was grounded.

What the Modernists learned about self, writing, authority, and representation in their highly fruitful interaction with journalism soon began to filter into their nonjournalistic work. However, this is more evident at the ideological than at the formal level. Formally as well as ideologically, the early Modernist poetry (of which Darío's *Prosas profanas* is the best example) presented itself as the epitome of harmony and control, "*un aire suave de pausados giros*"; yet there was an undercurrent of pessimism and uncertainty beneath the airy façade of this poetry that would become more and more evident as the old century drew to a close. That pessimism is usually attributed to the "influence" of *fin de siècle* decadentism, as well as to sociopolitical factors, but I believe it goes much deeper. It is also a consequence of the disturbing discovery, made by both the Modernists and the European decadentists at about the same time, that literature has no "essence," that it is, in Kantian terms, "purposiveness without purpose" (*Werke*, pp. 290–1). In his poem "Cantos de vida y esperanza" (1905), Darío speaks eloquently about "the horror of literature":

> Such was my intention, to make of my pure soul
> a star, a sonorous fountain,
> with the horror of literature,
> mad with twilight and with dawn.

> *Tal fue mi intento, hacer del alma pura*
> *mía, una estrella, una fuente sonora,*
> *con el horror de la literatura*
> *y loco de crepúsculo y de aurora.* (p. 630)

A good many of the poems Martí left unpublished at his death, later collected as *Versos libres* and *Flores del destierro*, reveal a disharmony and an existential anguish that, according to some critics, prefigures the tone and some of the imagery found in the Vanguardist poetry of César Vallejo.[15] Many more examples could be cited, but suffice it to recall the diminished sense of selfhood and authority evident in Modernist books of poetry as diverse as Darío's *Cantos de vida y esperanza* (1905; in which one finds his morbid "Lo fatal"), Lugones' *Lunario sentimental* (1909), and Herrera y Reissig's *La Torre de las Esfinges* (1909).

One must agree with Octavio Paz when he remarks that the uniqueness of Modernism resides in its being, simultaneously, Spanish America's Romanticism, Symbolism, and early Vanguardism (*Children of the Mire,* p. 88). The Modernists were quintessentially bookish writers; they probed the nature of literature as no other group of Spanish American writers has ever done. In this respect, their experience with journalism was clearly invaluable. It showed them the limits and limitations of the petty and archaic notion of literature they had learned from Romantic philology and gave them a glimpse of the powers and perils of writing. It also prefigured the increased interaction with the mass media that is one of the hallmarks of today's Spanish American fiction, from García Márquez and Vargas Llosa, to Sarduy, Puig, and Poniatowska.

6

Journalism and the ethics of writing: Borges, García Márquez, Vargas Llosa, Poniatowska

> *SOPHIST WALLOPS HAUGHTY HELEN*
> *SQUARE ON PROBOSCIS.*
> *SPARTANS GNASH MOLARS.*
> *ITHACANS VOW PEN IS CHAMP*
>
> James Joyce, *Ulysses* (1922)

> *One of the virtues for which I prefer Protestant nations to those of the Catholic tradition is their concern with ethics.*
>
> Jorge Luis Borges, prologue to
> *Elogio de la sombra* (1969)

> *[T]here is a peculiar and unexpected relation between the affirmation of a universal moral law and storytelling. It would seem that such a law would stand by itself and that its connection either to narration as such or to any particular narrative would be adventitious and superficial at best. Nevertheless . . . the moral law gives rise by an intrinsic necessity to storytelling, even if that storytelling in one way or another puts into question or subverts the moral law. Ethics and narration cannot be kept separate, though their relation is neither symmetrical nor harmonious.*
>
> J. Hillis Miller, *The Ethics of Reading* (1987), p. 2

For nineteenth-century Spanish American narrators, journalistic discourse went from an important auxiliary in their textual struggle for political and social modernization to an oppressive set of rules promoted by the institution of the press, which severely curtailed the writers' desire for greater artistic freedom. Such early-nineteenth-century writers as José Joaquín Fernández de Lizardi, Domingo Faustino Sarmiento, and Ricardo Palma, to mention three major figures, all saw journalistic discourse as an ally in the modernizing projects they variously set forth in such works as *El Periquillo Sarniento, Facundo,* and *Tradiciones peruanas.* In contrast the turn-of-the-century *modernistas* – Martí, Nájera, Darío, Casal, and many others – despite their reliance on journalism to earn a living, felt that journalism as an institution was totally opposed to the ideals of artistic autonomy and authorial dignity for which they strived. They sought to modernize Spanish-language literature not through a radical break with the Hispanic literary tradition, but by enriching that tradition with new European models; journalism, with its view of language as merchandise and its tendency to devalue fiction-writing, was seen as an obstacle to that task.

But the Modernists did not face squarely the dilemma presented by journalism's implicit criticism of narrative fiction. How could narrative fiction compete with a medium such as the newspaper, which offered its readers – through the technological wizardry of the telegraph and the transatlantic cable – detailed, factual, and gripping accounts of events that were taking place on the other side of the globe? How could it compete with the immediacy, speed, and truth-value of journalism? The solution to this impasse was achieved by the avant-garde writers and artists of the first two decades of the twentieth century, in Spanish America as well as in Europe.

Several key traits of avant-garde literature need to be remembered; the first is Ortega y Gasset's notorious characterization of avant-garde art as "dehumanized": that is to say, an art that no longer relies on human figures, perceptions, or emotions. Avant-garde literature is "dehumanized," for instance, because it removes the author from the privileged position he or she had occupied throughout the nineteenth century. The voice of the avant-garde poet, says Ortega, "disappears, becomes volatilized, and is turned into a purely anonymous voice that holds words up in the air; words which are the true protagonists of the lyrical enterprise" (p. 42). Avant-garde writing openly welcomed the demotion of the author, against which the Modernists struggled. Another important trait of avant-garde literature, which Ortega does not note, is its tendency to view language as a concrete, physical entity, occupying a volume in space: in other words, as writing, rather than sound.[1] Such a spatialization of language is clearly reflected in avant-garde European and Spanish American poetry of the early 1900s in such works as the French poet Guillaume Apollinaire's *Calli-grammes* (1916) or the Chilean poet Vicente Huidobro's book *Poemas árticos* (1918); it is also incorporated in seminal works of avant-garde narrative, from Joyce's *Ulysses* and *Finnegans Wake* (1939) to Dos Passos' *Manhattan Transfer* (1925) and *U.S.A.* (1930–6). In these and many other works, writers experimented with typography, with the spacing of letters and words on the page, and with the technique – invented by such cubist painters as Picasso and Braque – of the collage: juxtaposing newspaper clippings, photographs, and heterogeneous objects on a flat surface.

It does not require much interpretation to realize that many of the traits identified with avant-garde literature – the demotion of the author, the spatialization of language, the deliberate frivolity, the passion for novelty, action, and color, and the penchant for brevity and synthesis – are qualities it shares with or directly derives from journalism. Indeed, avant-garde writing at first seemed to embrace journalism wholeheartedly, finding in it an antidote to the old-fashioned, overly rhetorical forms of turn-of-the-century writing, as well as to the Symbolist and Spanish American Modernist notions of "art for art's sake." As Roger Shattuck points out in regard to the European artists of the period, "A sample of the real world erupts in the middle of a work of art and violates its separateness. . . . The newspaper clippings in cubist collages serve to link them to the surrounding world of events, and real fragments fill the poems of Max Jacob, Cendrars, and Reverdy" (p. 331).

Furthermore, as I remarked earlier, the Modernists wished to renew Spanish-language literature but were reluctant to break with tradition. The avant-garde writers had no such scruples. In consonance with the "nihilistic moment" Renato Poggioli sees in the avant-garde (p. 61), the Argentine Ultraists and *martinfierristas* of the early 1920s adhered to the aggressive reductiveness of Italian Futurism (Bellini, p. 354). The Ultraists in particular proclaimed their aesthetic principles as: "1. – *Reduction* of lyric to its primordial element: metaphor. 2. – *Crossing out* of mediocre phrases, connectives, and useless adjectives. 3. – *Abolition* of ornamental work, confessionalism, circumstantialism, preachiness, and affected nebulousness. 4. – *Synthesis* of two or more images in one, thus broadening their suggestiveness" (Bellini, p. 354; emphasis added). There is a remarkable resemblance between these reductive, utilitarian principles and the observations made a generation earlier by the Modernist José Enrique Rodó in his essay "Cómo ha de ser un diario" ("What a daily newspaper should be like," 1914), when he points out that good newspaper writing is based on the "Spencerian theory of style," which "reduces the secret of good literary form to an economy of attention" (p. 1201). For the avant-gardists, mimicking journalism and its devices seemed to offer the escape from literary tradition for which they yearned. And yet, as we shall see, this "contamination" of literature with journalism also had the effect of undermining journalism's claim to be fundamentally different from fiction.

Some of the clearest and most important examples of the process by which the avant-garde writers renewed their literature while simultaneously carrying out an implied critique of journalism are to be found in the work of the Argentine Jorge Luis Borges, who was himself one of the founders of Ultraism in Argentina in 1921. Two early works by Borges are particularly noteworthy in this regard: his collection of narratives, *Historia universal de la infamia* (*Universal History of Infamy*, 1935), and his short story "El acercamiento a Almotásim" ("The Approach to Almotasim," also from 1935). In its original version *Universal History of Infamy* (there is an expanded edition from 1954) consists of seven brief texts that were serialized in the Saturday supplement of the Buenos Aires newspaper *Crítica*, for which Borges worked as literary editor. These texts are essentially capsule biographies of famous delinquents from different epochs and parts of the globe: a slave trader from Mississippi named Lazarus Morell; a British imposter named Arthur Orton (alias Tom Castro); the widow Ching, a nineteenth-century Chinese female pirate; Monk Eastman, a turn-of-the-century New York gangster; Billy the Kid (whom Borges calls "the disinterested killer, Bill Harrigan"); Kotsuke no Suké, a treacherous Japanese samurai; and Hakim of Merv, a false Muslim prophet. With its numerous allusions to slavery, Africa and blacks in the Americas, *Universal History of Infamy* also shows the influence of avant-garde movements of the 1930s, such as the Harlem Renaissance and the Afro-Cuban Movement.

Universal History of Infamy's avant-gardism is also evident in the book's style and structure. These infamous biographies are told in a condensed, ironic, collagelike style which, according to Borges in his prologue to the 1935 edition, consists of "disparate enumerations, sudden breaks in continuity, and the reduction of a man's whole life to two or three scenes" (p. 7). Although Borges links his narrative style to the movies of von Sternberg, its highly synthetic and fragmentary nature is also clearly related to journalism. Furthermore, the very subject of the stories – famous crimes and criminals – is journalistic, and the tales abound in concrete, factual references (although, on closer inspection, some of these turn out to be spurious). To reinforce the impression of factualism, there is also a brief bibliography of sources at the end of the book.

Thus, at first glance, *Universal History of Infamy* appears to be little more than a rather sensational and lurid collection of crime stories, which, save for their evident display of erudition, would be at home in any modern supermarket tabloid. However, despite our contemporary tendency to regard tabloid newspapers mostly as works of fiction, they, like all other forms of journalism, still claim to tell the unvarnished truth. Borges' narratives in *Universal History of Infamy* also make this claim through their association with historiography (with a very Hegelian "Universal History," no less) and their concern with historically documented, if rather obscure, characters.

Borges himself, in the self-critical prologue to the 1954 edition of his book, denounced these narrations as "the irresponsible game of a timid man who did not dare to write stories and who instead amused himself by falsifying and distorting (perhaps without aesthetic justification) other people's stories" (p. 10). Indeed, all the biographies in the book deal with individuals who practiced treachery, imposture, and deceit to further their criminal aims; some, like Lazarus Morell and Hakim of Merv, were false redeemers or prophets, who achieved positions of authority through lying. The topic of falsehood runs through these stories, sowing the seed of doubt in their readers. The imposter Tom Castro, for instance, on the advice of his black associate Ebenezer Bogle, fooled the public and the press in 1867 by presenting himself as the heir to a wealthy English family (pp. 31–40). Why, then, should his readers believe Borges' own narrative? With its numerous examples of deceit and misunderstanding, *Universal History of Infamy* undermines the illusion of language's neutrality and transparency on which the truth-value of journalism is founded. Language is seen in these narratives to be an unreliable, treacherous medium that can be manipulated for all sorts of ends.

A further demonstration of the unreliability of language and the perils of accepting at face value the differences between journalistic and literary discourse is provided by Borges in his well-known short story "The Approach to Almotasim," found in his book *Ficciones* (*Fictions,* 1944). The story consists of a fake book review of a novel titled *The Approach to Al-Mu'tasim,* by a lawyer from Bombay named Mir Bahadur Ali. Book reviews, as is known, are a form of literary journalism, and they are assumed, like all journalism, to be truthful. What makes "The Approach to Almotasim" special is that it *was* originally published as a book review in *Sur,* the highly respected Buenos Aries literary journal, and was later reprinted in one of Borges' books of essays, *Historia de la eternidad* (*History of Eternity,* 1936). Borges' story follows all the conventions of the book review format, and even produces apocryphal quotes by a number of real-life English literary critics, commenting on the nonexistent Mir Bahadur Ali's equally nonexistent novel (*Ficciones,* p. 35). Borges' imposture was so credible that some Argentine readers actually tried to order the book in England (Borges, "An Autobiographical Essay," pp. 239–40).

The minor scandal produced by Borges' close imitation of journalistic discourse in "The Approach to Almotasim" served to underscore the arbitrary nature of the difference between the discourses of journalism and narrative fiction. Borges effectively showed that, in order to create the impression of truth, journalism depends on a number of rhetorical devices that are of literary origin, and that therefore journalism's presumed linguistic objectivity and closeness to the truth are merely an illusion, an imposture, a fiction.

In subsequent stories and essays, Borges continued to display his deep epistemological skepticism. In "Pierre Menard, Author of the *Quixote*," for example, he underlined the conventional nature of texts and their dependence on institutional or traditional contexts for interpretation, such as when the narrator copies the same fragment of Cervantes' *Don Quixote* twice, attributing the second version to Menard and reinterpreting it according to its new context (*Ficciones*, pp. 54–5). It was probably no coincidence that the passage from the *Quixote* Borges chose for this exegesis was one in which Cervantes refers to "truth, whose mother is history" (*Ficciones*, p. 54): Borges was in fact challenging the truth of history, or of any written account of "facts." In his essay "The Modesty of History" (1952), Borges noted that, in general, so-called historic days are usually fictitious, and that "one of the tasks of governments (especially in Italy, Germany, and Russia) has been to fabricate them or simulate them with an abundance of prior propaganda and relentless publicity. Such days, in which one can discern the influence of Cecil B. De Mille, are related less to history than to journalism" (*Otras Inquisiciones*, p. 229). In Borges' view, journalism is merely a clumsy way of circulating interpretations, usually erroneous ones, about a reality that is fundamentally unknowable. The "modest history" Borges proposes in his essay is, in the end, none other than the history of writing, of representation: "Not the day when the Saxon said the words [Borges refers to an episode in the *Heimskringla*], but the day when an enemy perpetuated them, was the historic date" (*Otras Inquisiones*, p. 233). The closest thing to a "true history" would be, as Borges states in another essay, "Pascal's Sphere" (1951), "the history of the diverse intonation of a few metaphors" (*Otras Inquisiones*, p. 17).

The tenor of Borges' criticism of historical and, by extension, journalistic discourse is similar to Friedrich Nietzsche's more general critique of language's truth-value. In a well-known passage of his *Philosophenbuch* (1875), Nietzsche asks:

What, then, is truth? A mobile army of metaphors, metonyms, and anthropomorphisms – in short, a sum of human relations, which have been enhanced, transposed, and embellished poetically and rhetorically, and which after long use seem firm, canonical, and obligatory to a people: truths are illusions about which one has forgotten that this is what they are; metaphors which are worn out and without sensuous power; coins which have lost their pictures and now matter only as metal, no longer as coins. (pp. 180–2)

Thus, the avant-garde's apparent embrace of journalism actually concealed a strategy to undermine the ideological prestige and power of journalistic discourse, a prestige and power based on journalism's supposed ability to become a transparent medium for facts. Once this critique was performed, Spanish American writers could again, as before the turn of the century, deal with journalism on an equal footing.

This did not mean, of course, a return to such nineteenth-century notions as the supremacy of the author. Although the Spanish American *novelas de la tierra,* such as Ricardo Güiraldes' *Don Segundo Sombra* (1926) or Rómulo Gallegos' *Doña Bárbara* (1929), which were contemporary to the avant-garde, might superficially seem to be throwbacks to nineteenth-century narrative realism, recent criticism has shown them to be semiotically sophisticated works, whose authors wrote with a deep awareness of the unreliability of language and the doubtful status of the author in modern literature.[2] Following Borges' and the avant-garde's epistemological critique of journalism, other precursors of the "boom" period, such as Alejo Carpentier, as well as the novelists of the "boom" themselves, carried out a further demolition of the hierarchical difference between journalistic and fictional discourses. Often, as in Carpentier's case, this demolition was part of a broader exploration of the links between narrative fiction and historical discourse.[3]

In general, in today's Spanish American narrative (from the "boom" to the "postboom"), journalistic discourse is assimilated quite freely and openly as one of many elements in a textual repertoire that contributes to the narrative. This does not mean that journalism is no longer significant in fictional narrative; rather, whenever journalism is alluded to or otherwise "grafted" onto the fictional text, its significance becomes more complex and varied. Its presence in the text no longer implies – as frequently occurred during the nineteenth century – that the text is being "truthful" or that it proposes a modernizing agenda. Even in today's documentary novels the role of journalism as an emblem of truth and modernity in the text is problematized.

However, I believe the various avatars of journalistic discourse in contemporary Spanish American fiction still have something in common: their connection to ethics. In recent Spanish American fiction, I propose, the use of journalistic discourse, or journalism's presence as a motif, is always linked to ethical or moral considerations. The definition of "ethics" I have found most persuasive and useful in the context of literary criticism is the one proposed by Paul de Man in *Allegories of Reading* (1979). Availing himself of Kantian terminology even as he disagrees with Kant, de Man defines ethics as "the structural interference of two distinct value systems" and he adds: "the ethical category is imperative (i.e., a category rather than a value) to the extent that it is linguistic and not subjective. . . . The passage to an ethical tonality does not result from a transcendental imperative but is the referential (and therefore unreliable) version of a linguistic confusion. Ethics (or, one should say ethicity) is a discursive mode among others" (p. 206). For de Man, ethics is fundamentally a function of language, not of any transcendental principle (such as God, reason, or society). It arises whenever different value systems meet and clash, and each side feels the need to reaffirm its principles.

Later in this chapter I present concrete examples of this in several important Spanish American novels. Before doing so, however, I will review the circumstances which have led to the Spanish American narrators' return to ethics in the 1980s. This return to ethics is primarily a function of the narrators' continuing importance in their societies and their greater access to journalism and the media. Unlike their counterparts of earlier decades, who were often regarded as journalists first and fiction writers second, the Spanish American narrators' current involvement with the press usually casts them in a special role: that of the intellectual celebrity-commentator, a cultural pundit whose insights are less important than the person from whom they emanate. "Grandes Firmas" ("Great Signatures"), the title of a syndicated series of articles by major Hispanic writers, distributed by the Spanish press agency EFE during the 1980s, is suggestive in this regard. Unlike many of their Romantic and Modernist precursors, today's narrators are given broad latitude to write what they please, as they please, within the normal limitations of space in print journalism.[4] With greater freedom and authority, with a stronger voice in journalism and the media, and no longer quite so marginalized in their societies, Spanish American writers have increasingly felt the burdens and responsibilities of their prominence (Mario Vargas Llosa's failed run for the presidency of Peru in 1990 is perhaps the most extreme instance of this phenomenon). It is not surprising, then, that ethical concerns – which had been banished from most nonpropagandistic fiction since the telluric novels of the 1930s – have returned to the Spanish American narrative.

Journalism is an appropriate vehicle for such a return, since, like medicine and the law, it is generally conceived of as a public service, and possesses a rich and varied repertoire of ethical reflection. Working within the Western philosophical tradition, which equates truth with goodness, journalism as an institution regards itself as the bearer of deeply cherished moral values, despite abundant evidence of its frequent axiological neutrality and its submission to the profit motive. In fact, as the Spanish American Modernists realized to their dismay (see Chapter 5), textuality, money, and power intersect far more visibly and literally in journalism than in literature. Precisely because of journalism's all-too-frequent nearness to "the powers that be," there have been numerous attempts in the United States and Latin America to formulate journalistic codes of ethics analogous to the physicians' Hippocratic Oath.[5] As the influence of religious discourse waned, the secular character of journalistic ethics probably also added to its attractiveness for modern writers. The narrators and journalists of nineteenth-century Spanish America, although they might be unbelievers, still posed ethical questions in a language fraught with religious overtones: Among many examples, we may recall Ricardo Palma's frequent allusions to the Devil as an emblem of social satire in his *Tradiciones peruanas*.[6] Contemporary Spanish American fiction, however, in works such as Cortázar's *Libro de Manuel* (*Manual for Manuel*, 1973), Vargas Llosa's *La tía Julia y el escribidor* (*Aunt Julia and the Scriptwriter*, 1977), and García Márquez's *Crónica de una muerte anunciada* (*Chronicle of a Death Foretold*, 1981), has largely substituted religious discourse with journalism as a textual marker for ethical or moral issues. Instead of the priest, it is now the journalist who confronts moral questions and anguishes over them, and in a language that is predominantly secular and philosophical rather than religious.

In addition to general moral concerns dealing with "good" and "evil" in society, journalism has injected into contemporary Spanish American narrative what I would call an "ethics of writing."[7] I do not mean to suggest that earlier Spanish American writers were unconcerned with the ethical issues of their profession, but that until recently such a concern was usually mediated by ideology: Ideologies, whether from the left or right, tended to dictate the writers' relation to their society and to their work. The "ethics of writing" is a more encompassing phenomenon and, above all, is imbued with a critical, philosophical spirit. Instead of a catalogue of moral injunctions about the writers' responsibility to society (as one finds in nineteenth-century literary criticism as well as in twentieth-century Marxist criticism), the contemporary ethics of writing is an attempt by the writers themselves to figure out the moral implications of their work. Instead of commandments and principles, this ethics of writing formulates questions – questions for which there are no simple, dogmatic answers, such as: What does it mean to be a writer in countries where the vast majority of the population is illiterate? Does fiction-writing tend to be complicitous with the sources of social and political oppression, or is it, on the contrary, an inherently subversive, antiauthoritarian activity? Can one truly write "beyond good and evil," or does all fiction contain implicit moral judgments? These are but a few of the ethical queries raised by recent Spanish-American fiction through the mediation of journalistic discourse.

To test this hypothesis, let us briefly examine three outstanding examples of the various ways journalistic discourse and ethics interact in today's Spanish American novel. The roster of contemporary Spanish American writers who have practiced journalism and have visibly incorporated it into their novels is extensive, but I will limit my comments in the remainder of this chapter to works by Gabriel García Márquez, Mario Vargas Llosa, and Elena Poniatowska.

Much has been written about García Márquez's journalistic oeuvre, but little about its impact on his literary work. At most, journalism has been viewed as a thematic source for some of

García Márquez's narratives, or as a recurrent motif in his work, but few critics have reflected on journalism's *significance* as a leitmotiv, that is, on the meaning of the thematic inclusion of journalism in García Márquez's novels and stories.[8] I have elsewhere attempted to do this in some detail; rather than merely summarize the conclusions of my previous work, I would like to use it as a point of departure for some further thoughts on how (and what) journalism signifies in García Márquez's texts.

There are allusions to journalism in several works by García Márquez, such as *In Evil Hour* (1961), *One Hundred Years of Solitude* (1967), *The Autumn of the Patriarch* (1975), and *Love in the Time of Cholera* (1985); he has also published reportages with a strong novelistic character in the vein of the documentary novel, such as *The Story of a Shipwrecked Sailor* (1970) and *Clandestine in Chile: The Adventures of Miguel Littín* (1987).[9] But two key fictional texts in which journalism forms the narrative's backbone are his short story "Big Mama's Funeral" (1962) and his novel *Chronicle of a Death Foretold.* These two texts exemplify what I consider to be changes in García Márquez's thoughts about journalism, its role in society, and its relationship to fiction.[10]

In "Big Mama's Funeral," journalism is viewed, in a rather conventional fashion, as a liberating practice, and freedom of the press is paralleled with the liberation of literature from the shackles of an old-fashioned rhetoricism. An apocryphal obituary, the story's effectiveness depends almost entirely on the narrator's parody of the bombastic rhetoric of journalistic sensationalism:

This is, for all the world's unbelievers, the true account of Big Mama, absolute sovereign of the Kingdom of Macondo, who lived in possession of power for ninety-two years, and died in the odor of sanctity one Tuesday last September, and whose funeral was attended by the Pope. (*Los funerales,* p. 131)

In an antigenealogical gesture reminiscent of Palma's *Tradiciones peruanas,* the account of Big Mama's death signals the end of an autarchic, genealogy-obsessed idea of language and the beginning of the antigenealogical, decentered age of writing.[11] While alive, Big Mama sought to control language absolutely by systematically erasing the conventional boundaries of "propriety/property" that coordinate meaning, while using her power to impose her own order and ensure the continuity and cohesion of her bloodline (*Los funerales*, pp. 133, 139). For example, although she was a virgin, Big Mama decided who among her relatives was going to marry whom (*Los funerales*, p. 136, 137). It is only fitting that, after her death, when she is no longer present to enforce her interpretation of the codes (legal and linguistic) on which she based her power, a carnivalesque, disseminating festivity should ensue (*Los funerales*, pp. 148–50), and that all these events should be narrated in the rhetoric of a textual institution that has made of dissemination its byword: journalism.[12] The story's recourse to journalism's immediacy and penchant for detail becomes a liberating gesture after the endless years of Big Mama's stultifying ideological abstractions: "The wealth of the subsoil, the territorial waters, the colors of the flag, national sovereignty, the traditional parties, the rights of man, civil rights, the nation's leadership, the right of appeal, Congressional hearings, letters of recommendation, historical records, free elections, beauty queens . . . ," etcetera (*Los funerales*, p. 141).

Journalism in the story is a demystifying practice, not only at the social level (as in the cliché of the valiant journalist exposing corruption in government), but also at the textual level. Unlike the other, more "exalted" discourses to which Big Mama resorted, with their vacuous and high-sounding phrases, the discourse of journalism deals with the everyday, the ordinary, and even the excremental. Journalism's emphasis on empirical details and its (rather deluded) belief in its own veracity mock and corrode the abstract and totalizing impulse of a certain literary language that is symbolized in the story by Big Mama.

In *Chronicle of a Death Foretold*, however, García Márquez's view of journalism is much more problematic and considerably less optimistic. This novel, like *One Hundred Years of Solitude*, involves the decipherment and interpretation of events; like *In Evil Hour* and "Big Mama's Funeral," it deals with the attributes and limitations of authority, in the political as well as the literary sense of the term. But if in "Big Mama's Funeral" journalism stood for a carnivalesque textual liberation, here it becomes a grim Borgesian labyrinth: The exultation of freedom is replaced by the burden of interpretation, of making sense out of reality's chaos. And this is where ethics comes in, as a consequence of journalism's perennial search for the truth.

In *Chronicle of a Death Foretold*, the narrator–protagonist is a journalist who returns to his hometown to investigate a very public, execution-style murder that had taken place there more than twenty years before. As the narrator attempts to piece together the story – which is as fragmented as the victim's mutilated body – of the murder of the wealthy and seductive Santiago Nasar, he also tries to assess the collective responsibility of the townspeople in Nasar's murder. A *"why*dunit" more than a "whodunit" (since the identity of the killers is known, and they have been tried for their crime), the novel dwells on the innumerable inconsistencies, lapses of memory, and outright falsehoods in the many versions of Santiago Nasar's murder: Why did Santiago not heed the many warnings of his impending doom? Why wasn't anyone in the town able to stop the Vicario twins from murdering Santiago? Why did Angela Vicario choose to accuse Santiago Nasar of deflowering her? Why did her brothers believe her, when there were doubts about her story?

This emphasis on the processal aspects of journalism is a departure in *Chronicle of a Death Foretold;* the novel is less a parody of journalistic rhetoric (although there is some of this in the text) than a scale model of the process of journalistic investigation. Through this process, García Márquez unveils the role played by causality, chance, and manipulation in both journalism and narrative fiction. The event that gives rise to the story in *Chronicle of a Death Foretold* may be classified as a *fait-divers*, which, to repeat Roland Barthes' definition, is a news story in which the event somehow violates our normal expectations of causality and in which coincidence plays an important role.[13] The *fait-divers* is probably the most "literary" form of news, because the reverse causality, the coincidences and ironies which that type of journalism emphasizes all resemble a deliberate manipulation of events by an unknown author, by – as Barthes puts it – a "god [that] prowls behind the *fait-divers*" (*Critical Essays*, p. 114). The paradoxical, *fait-divers*-like nature of the story is evident from the start: Santiago Nasar was murdered in full sight of the townspeople, by two friends who did not really want to kill him and who did all they could to make someone stop them.

The novel's narrator is fascinated by causality and the questions it raises. Like José Arcadio Buendía trying to find God by taking daguerreotype pictures of everything in Macondo, the narrator in *Chronicle of a Death Foretold* tries to find Barthes' "god that prowls behind the *fait-divers*," that is, the controlling principle that produces the narrative and gives it the illusion of coherence. The narrator, however, is well aware that his own control over his narrative is as feeble and uncertain as that of the anonymous magistrate who first investigated the case, whose "good work at times seemed ruined by disillusionment" (*Crónica*, p. 131), and who "never thought it legitimate that life should make use of so many coincidences forbidden to literature" (*Crónica*, p. 130). Paradoxically, the narrator's seeming lack of control is quite deliberate, as I argue below.

In his seminal essay, "Narrative Art and Magic" (1932), Borges posited an absolute or "magical" causality as one of the key elements in narrative fiction: According to Borges, causality in the novel is anti-Aristotelian; instead of a clear-cut linear sequence of events linked by an original cause or Prime Mover, novelistic causality irradiates from all the elements in the story and in all directions, so that, in a well-constructed novel, everything and anything can be significant, everything forms a part of a "rigorous scheme of attentions, echoes, and affinities" (*Discusión*, p. 90). In *Chronicle of a Death Foretold*, García Márquez turns Borges' lucid exposition inside-out, and shows that it is virtually impossible to generate such a "rigorous scheme of attentions, echoes, and affinities" out of the chaotic multiplicity of the real world without resorting to dishonesty and deceit. The Colombian author is not merely repeating Borges' well-known contention that narrative is always a fiction, but is also placing that assertion in the context of an ethics of writing. If to narrate is to lie, and if narrators are always part of a larger social milieu, then what is their place in society? To what standards should they be held accountable? Are they merely innocent entertainers? Or are they, despite their best intentions, like Borges' con men in *Universal History of Infamy*, beings who play with and prey upon their readers' judgment in order to achieve their aims?

In what seems almost a literal version of de Man's abstract definition, the ethical dimension of *Chronicle of a Death Foretold* arises from the conflict and confusion of two distinct value-systems: The Christian one, which preaches mercy and forgiveness, and the more ancient Mediterranean code of honor, which demands vengeance for real or perceived stains upon the family name. The need to understand how such a confusion could have led to a man's death leads the narrator toward broader ethical questions bearing on authority, fiction, and journalism, which in turn give this novel its particular poignancy. The novel strongly suggests that, for multiple and sometimes conflicting reasons, the townspeople sanctioned the killing of Santiago Nasar. Clearly, Santiago's death as a scapegoat simplified matters for almost everyone in the town. Among other things, it avoided a judicial inquiry about Angela Vicario's lost virginity, an inquiry that might have raised serious questions about more than one of the townspeople's morals (for instance, other than the priest, men in the town seemed to be customers of María Alejandrina Cervantes' bordello), and might have undone the fragile social fictions that held the town together. The parallels between this incident and the traditional Hispanic Holy Week Passion Play, as well as classical Spanish dramas such as Lope de Vega's *Fuenteovejuna* (1612), are obvious, and, along with many other details in the text, they point to a link between violence, authority, and narrative.[14] García Márquez suggests that the coherence and clarity associated with political as well as narrative authority always emanate from an arbitrary, irrational, sometimes violent act, an act exactly parallel to the institution of moral principles, the "Thou shalls" or "Thou shall nots" with which one can neither reason nor dispute.

In any case, García Márquez reminds us, authority – be it political or literary – can never escape judgment, and, when judged, may sometimes be found wanting. Therefore, like the canniest of journalists, the narrator of *Chronicle of a Death Foretold* shrewdly seeks to avoid the burden of authority, of simplifying matters in his attempt to narrate them. To do this, the narrator neither excises coincidence from his tale nor attempts to explain it; instead, he incorporates causality and chance into his text in such a visible way that he leaves his critics with nothing solid at which to strike – just a handful of pages from a flooded legal file (*Crónica*, p. 129) and a bundle of conflicting interpretations.

The world of narrative, as it appears in this novel, is without a single, all-powerful "God" or authority figure. Rather, it is populated, like the cosmos of Greek myth, with numberless minor deities, each vying for a share of power in the text, each adding one voice to the constant background hubbub from which the narrative springs.[15] Through his canny use of journalistic discourse in *Chronicle of a Death Foretold*, García Márquez reveals the humble, threadbare origins of narrative in gossip, conjecture, and the petty details of life, as well as narrative's dependence on belief – on "prejudice" as the unnamed magistrate says (*Crónica*, p. 131) – to achieve the authority and power it wields over its readers.

The topic of journalism is similarly linked to questions of literary and ethical import in novels by Mario Vargas Llosa as different as *Aunt Julia and the Scriptwriter* and *La guerra del fin del mundo* (*The War of the End of the World*, 1981). Vargas Llosa is renowned as the author of stylistically sophisticated realist fiction in the tradition of the French novelist Gustave Flaubert. Although the style of his novels abounds in complex temporal and spatial dislocations derived from the avant-garde legacy of Joyce, Dos Passos, and Faulkner, Vargas Llosa is nevertheless one of the many twentieth-century writers who see Flaubert as the first Modernist, as a precursor of the avant-garde.[16] Furthermore, like Flaubert's, Vargas Llosa's novels are written after a process of careful and scrupulous documentation akin to the research done by a journalist when following a story.

Another French writer's impact on Vargas Llosa's literary ideology has been almost as great as Flaubert's: Jean-Paul Sartre. Indeed, Vargas Llosa's *oeuvre* may be seen a typically Spanish-American attempt to fuse and reconcile opposing views of literature, in this case, Flaubert's amoral aestheticism with Sartre's well-known view of literature as a *prise de position*.[17] Critics have taken note of this and, while recognizing Vargas Llosa's Flaubertian concern with narrative technique, some, like Lafforgue, have also categorized him as a "moralist."

It is probably the tension between Vargas Llosa's Flaubertian preoccupation with narrative technique and his Sartrean sense of moral responsibility that explains why in *Aunt Julia and the Scriptwriter* and *The War of the End of the World* journalism is viewed in a negative light, as a failed attempt to master the complexities of reality through writing. Journalists are seen by Vargas Llosa either as immature, naive transcribers of information, or as prejudiced providers of one-sided stories. Immaturity is a salient trait of Marito, the protagonist of *Aunt Julia and the Scriptwriter,* a novel which may be considered Vargas Llosa's analogue to Joyce's *Portrait of the Artist as a Young Man* (1916). Marito, who edits the news read over Radio Panamericana and dreams of becoming a great writer like Maupassant, Somerset Maugham, or Borges (his models change almost daily), is nevertheless fascinated by the figure of Pedro Camacho, a scriptwriter, producer, and director of radio soap operas. Camacho's abundant production, unbridled imagination, devotion to his craft, and immense popularity seem to mock Marito's feeble attempts at writing fiction like one of the "great masters." Ultimately, Marito learns that, in order to become more than a mere scribbler, he must try to unite and balance Pedro Camacho's craftsmanship and imagination with his own social and moral commitment.[18]

In the second instance, the character of the myopic journalist in *The War of the End of the World,* loosely based on the real-life Brazilian journalist Euclides Da Cunha, is the exception that proves the rule. The character's physical myopia forces him, quite unexpectedly, to perceive and narrate the events of Canudos in a deeper fashion (Bernucci, pp. 85–7): "Everybody laughs [the myopic journalist says] when I tell them I didn't see what happened in Canudos because I broke my glasses (. . .) But even though I didn't see them, I felt, heard, smelled the things that happened. . . . And I intuitively sensed the rest" (*The War . . .* , p. 340). Because of his reliance on intuition and imagination, and also because of his sensitivity to ethical concerns, the myopic journalist was able to narrate the story of the backlands religious uprising more faithfully and evenhandedly than the other war correspondents who "could see and yet they didn't see. All they saw was what they'd come to see. Even if there was no such thing there." (p. 394).

In both cases, Vargas Llosa implies that the discourse of journalism is too rigid and constrained to adequately convey the nuances of experience. Vargas Llosa inverts the usual distinctions between journalism and fiction, which view journalism as empirical and fiction tending toward idealization. For Vargas Llosa, journalism is too abstract and formulaic, whereas novels offer richer, more concrete, and more detailed versions of experience. As he states in his essay, "La verdad de las mentiras" ("The Truth of Lies," 1989): "Fiction is a temporary substitution of life. The return to reality is always a brutal impoverishment: a confirmation that we are less than what we dream" (pp. 12–13). Nevertheless, journalism is still associated in Vargas Llosa's work with the genesis of the novelistic text as a source of raw material, of stories, whose often schematic nature the novelist supplements with his own observations of the gritty texture of reality.

Vargas Llosa's view of journalistic discourse as paradoxically less truthful than fiction seems to suggest that, to him, journalism is inherently unethical. Yet, whatever his opinions may be in this regard, in the above-mentioned novels journalism clearly forms a part of the narrative's ethical interrogations. For example, in *Aunt Julia and the Scriptwriter,* Marito plagiarizes and rewrites news stories so that they can be read as bulletins over Radio Panamericana: "I had a job with a pompous title, modest salary, illegal appropriations, and flexible hours: Director of Information of Radio Panamericana. It consisted in cutting out the interesting news items which appeared in the newspapers, and making them up a little [*maquillarlas un poco*] so that they could be read as news bulletins" (p. 11). This process is analogous to Vargas Llosa's rewriting of his own biography in the novel as a whole; the writing of *Aunt Julia and the Scriptwriter* also entails a sort of textual *maquillaje* (in more ways than one, since one of the main characters, Aunt Julia, is a woman and another, Pedro Camacho, is an actor as well as a scriptwriter), and this "make-up" turns what was an old story into a new one: the novel itself. And the story the novel tells, its "news," – which is sensational and melodramatic, like the bulletins Pascual (Marito's assistant) likes to put on the air and, of course, like Pedro Camacho's soap operas – clearly has moral implications, since Marito and Aunt Julia choose to transgress familial and social codes by marrying. Moreover, since the novel also deals with Marito's learning how to become a writer, issues related to

the ethics of writing are also explored: the relation between
fiction and social reality, the value and validity of genre distinctions, and the link between authority and transgression.

The War of the End of the World dramatizes these issues quite
clearly in a text that seamlessly weaves the elements of journalistic discourse, melodrama, and history that are kept separate in *Aunt Julia's* parallelistic structure. The text of the novel
itself emanates from something that was originally journalistic
reportage, Euclides da Cunha's masterpiece, *Os Sertões* (1902).
Da Cunha's work, like Sarmiento's *Facundo*, is a potent mixture
of narration, analysis, and sensationalism that inquires into the
conflictive forces behind Brazilian nationhood. Vargas Llosa's
novel is a metahistorical rewriting of *Os Sertões* that questions da
Cunha's questions; that is, it focuses as much on the incidents of
the Canudos rebellion (which is the subject of *Os Sertões*) as on
the problematics of writing about it. I have already mentioned
the character of the myopic journalist, whose sensitivity to the
ethical issues underlying Antonio Conselheiro's uprising allows
him to report more faithfully on the events; but there are other,
less successful author-figures in the text: There is the illiterate
Conselheiro himself, whose *dicta* are written down by León de
Natuba, a physically deformed follower; there is Galileo Gall,
the anarchist and phrenologist who attempts to publish his
ideas in a Lyons newspaper titled *L'Etincelle de la révolte* (The
Spark of Rebellion), and, lastly, there is the Dwarf, an oral narrator who retells popular romances.

In certain respects, *The War of the End of the World* reads like a
vastly expanded rewriting of *Chronicle of a Death Foretold*. The
crushing defeat of the Canudos rebellion at the hands of the
Brazilian army and the death of Santiago Nasar share an air of
inevitability. There is, furthermore, a plurality of versions
about the events that transpired, and, as I have indicated, a
plurality of narrators, although the latter appears subsumed in
an omniscient narrative voice – unlike that of the narrator in
García Márquez's novel, who is himself a character in the text
and does not have access to all the facts. The narrator's omni-
science in *The War of the End of the World*, however, is less than it
appears, since he deliberately avoids any attempt at interpreting the events, and allows the coexistence of other chroniclers.
Also similar are the collective nature of the events and the

Biblical parallelisms, which in Vargas Llosa's novel are even more explicit. Religion, as can be seen, is not absent from these novels, but is simply one code, one discourse among others.

In the struggle of the fanatically religious *jagunços* against the positivistic Brazilian state, we again find a clash of opposing values, a clash that is resolved in the mass sacrifice of thousands of human beings. As in *Chronicle of a Death Foretold,* Vargas Llosa's novel poses key questions for an ethics of writing: How to narrate against authority? How to avoid repeating in the narrative (as Sarmiento did in *Facundo* in the 1850s) the oppressive mechanisms the narrative is meant to denounce? Paradoxically, like García Márquez, Vargas Llosa seeks refuge from this dilemma in a detached and ironic stance similar to Flaubert's (particularly in novels like *Salammbô,* 1862) – one that is very much like that of the journalists whom Vargas Llosa professes to distrust. Clearly, the aim of these writers as narrators is not to intervene, or even to judge, but to question and attempt to understand.

The ironic stance is strenuously avoided by writers of documentary fiction, a genre in which the Mexican Elena Poniatowska has produced important and intriguing works.[19] The Spanish American documentary novel, although inspired by the anthropological technique of the "life history" as well as by the "New Journalism" of U.S. writers such as Tom Wolfe and Norman Mailer, is far closer to the tradition of nineteenth-century narratives in which journalism and fiction were thoroughly – and strategically – mixed. This tradition includes the works I have discussed earlier, such as *El Periquillo Sarniento, Facundo, Tradiciones peruanas,* and the Modernist chronicles, as well as a diverse group of texts that might be analyzed in a similar fashion: the *Autobiografía* (1835) by Cuban slave Juan Francisco Manzano, *Una excursión a los indios Ranqueles* (1872) by Argentine Lucio V. Mansilla, *Mis memorias* (1882) by Puerto Rican Alejandro Tapia y Rivera, *Los bandidos de Río Frío* (1891) by Mexican Manuel Payno, and many others. Like those nineteenth-century texts, today's documentary narratives attest to their authors' intensely personal involvement with the social and political issues of their day.

Elena Poniatowska's *Hasta no verte, Jesús mío* (*Until I See You, My Jesus,* 1969) and *La noche de Tlatelolco* (*Massacre in Mexico,*

1971) are two of the most ambitious and sophisticated examples of contemporary documentary fiction in Spanish America.[20] In both, the figure of the journalist is important, although
it remains hidden in the background in *Hasta no verte, Jesús mío*,
and appears in *Massacre in Mexico* as a mere editor and transcriber of the voices and documents featured in the text. Imbued
with social purpose and a sense of indignation, contemporary
documentary fiction presents itself primarily as a nonliterary,
direct transcription of the human voice, particularly the voices
of those who have been marginalized by society, such as Jesusa
Palancares in *Hasta no verte, Jesús mío* and the protesters in *Massacre in Mexico*. Like journalism, documentary fiction attempts
to create an impression of immediacy by turning language into
a straightforward, transparent medium of communication.

But it is not so simple to escape from fiction. Contemporary
notions of what is "fictional" are quite broad, and encompass
what once were nonfictional elements. Also, once a text is written, it leaves itself open to comparison with fictional works
from the literary tradition, and there is a strong tendency to
assimilate it into that tradition: For example, critics have
pointed out the close similarities between documentary narratives such as *Hasta no verte, Jesús mío* and Miguel Barnet's *The
Autobiography of a Runaway Slave* (1966) with the tradition of the
picaresque novel (Kerr, p. 374; González Echevarría, *The Voice
of the Masters*, p. 121). Moreover, within the text of *Hasta no verte,
Jesus mío* the old, poverty-stricken Jesusa Palancares refuses to
become Poniatowska's docile "informant"; her willful, essentially authorial personality comes through in her words, particularly in the many segments in which Jesusa speaks of her
spiritualist beliefs and dreams. In those sections, her narrative
– which is in fact a composite of her voice and Poniatowska's –
becomes highly metaphorical and inventive; the richness and
vitality of her lower-class Spanish, rendered by Poniatowska in
minute and loving detail, calls attention to itself in a manner
that far exceeds the requirements of either anthropology or
journalism.

Critics have also noted how the claims of truthfulness made
by the text of *Hasta no verte, Jesús mío*, as well as by the character
of Jesusa herself, are put into question by Jesusa's own implicit
theory about truth and falsehood (Kerr, p. 375). A telling pas-

sage in this regard is the novel's epigraph, in which Jesusa speaks proleptically about the end of her story and of her death:

One day you'll come and you won't find me; you'll just find the wind alone. When that day comes, there'll be no one to tell you what became of me. And you'll think it was all a lie. It's true, our life is just a lie [*Es verdad, estamos aquí de a mentiras*]: what they tell over the radio is just lies, lies are what the neighbors say and what you say about missing me is just lies [*lo que cuentan en el radio son mentiras, mentiras las que dicen los vecinos y mentira que me va a sentir*]. If I'm no use to you anymore, why the hell are you going to miss me? And in the workshop too. Who do you think is going to miss me when I won't even say goodbye? (p. 8)

In a sense, Poniatowska has created in Jesusa a version of the "Cretan Liar" paradox: "All Cretan are liars," says a Cretan.[21] This proposition, which is inherently undecidable in terms of its truth or falsehood, may be considered a scale model of the underlying problematics of documentary fiction: These texts purport to speak about the "real world," but their veracity depends almost totally on the degree of reliability we assign to the narrator. Such reliability seems minimal, at best, given the "authorial duplicity" of documentary narratives, a duplicity which raises questions as to who is the text's "true" author: Elena, or Jesusa, or both (Kerr, p. 372; González Echevarría, *The Voice of the Masters*, pp. 121–2).

A similar phenomenon occurs in *Massacre in Mexico* (original title *La noche de Tlatelolco*), a textual collage of quotes from eyewitnesses of the 1968 Tlatelolco massacre, plus photographs, newspaper editorials and articles, political slogans, protest songs, and even poems by such authors as Rosario Castellanos and Octavio Paz (in Poniatowska, *La noche de Tlatelolco*, pp. 163–4, 268 respectively). Once again, the unruly vitality of fiction and imagination emanates from what were supposed to be simple transcriptions of oral and written testimonies, with the added twist that questioning the text's veracity puts one in the undesirable moral position of seeming to condone the Mexican government's unspeakable brutality. How does one perform literary criticism on texts such as the following without feeling an accomplice to the killing?

We went from one floor to another and, in the central section of the Chihuahua building, I don't recall on which floor, I felt something sticky beneath my feet. I turned and saw blood, a lot of blood, and I told my husband: "Look, Carlos, how much blood, there was a slaughter here!" Then one of the corporals spoke to me: "Heck, ma'am, you sure don't know blood, because you see a little and make such a fuss!" But there was a lot, a lot of blood, so much that I felt in my hand the viscousness of blood. There was also blood on the walls; I think the walls of Tlatelolco have their pores full of blood. The whole of Tlatelolco reeks of blood. More than one person bled to death there, because it was too much blood for one person.

Margarita Nolasco, anthropologist (in Poniatowska, *La noche de Tlatelolco*, p. 171)

Here the lessons taught by García Márquez's *Chronicle of a Death Foretold* and Vargas Llosa's *The War of the End of the World* come to the fore: The ethical dimension is inescapable in any narrative that purports to communicate the truth, and a certain degree of a priori faith must be placed in the text so that it becomes coherent and credible. Documentary narratives, like journalism, are profoundly ethical in that their stories are built around moral imperatives; one of these is *Thou shalt not lie.* (From the reader's standpoint, this particular imperative translates as *Thou shalt not doubt.*) Despite their pretense at objectivity, moralism is pervasive in the documentary narratives, since, like melodrama (to which many of these texts recur), they always deal with fundamental polar oppositions (Brooks, p. 4): truth *versus* falsehood, justice *versus* injustice, society *versus* the individual. With the best intentions, documentary texts often manipulate their readers' emotions, forcing them to judge or be judged, to accept the narrative at face value or risk moral opprobrium.[22] Enactments of undecidability – like the "Cretan Liar" paradox – documentary narratives nevertheless impose upon the reader the burden of making a moral choice, partly because they make ethically unacceptable the option to read them as fiction. If García Márquez and Vargas Llosa, following Borges, regard the author as a morally dubious figure – part dictator, part con man – documentary narratives transfer that burden to the reader. Before them, the reader is left like the protagonist of Kafka's parable, "Before the Law": standing hesitantly before the gates to the Law, waiting for someone else to be the first to enter, only to realize at the end that the gates were meant for him alone, and now they are closed. This parable has generally been interpreted as an illustration of the enigmatic, self-sufficient nature of literature, which is, so to speak, "a law unto itself." Despite their rejection of literature, documentary narratives are still constituted in relation to literary principles. Although they pretend to be as naively referential as journalism or as Kafka's text, documentary narratives in fact present their readers with daunting and probably irresolvable moral dilemmas. Like the open doorway to the Law in Kafka's tale, they present an open, highly readable façade, but this openness is always guarded, watched over – in Kafka, by a fearsome doorman, in documentary narrative by their underlying "Cretan Liar" paradox. In either case, the text seems to invite access (to the Law, to meaning) but actually withholds it.[23]

Poniatowska's documentary narratives, like the fictions of García Márquez and Vargas Llosa, utilize journalistic discourse in two apparently disparate ways: one, as an instrument for an anthropological inquiry into the roots of national culture, and the other, as a way to return to the very foundations of Spanish American narrative – foundations that were laid in the conflict and mingling of disparate discourses during the nineteenth century. Both approaches, however, are aspects of the same modern search for beginnings, for origins, a search that inevitably begins with the profoundly journalistic attempt to identify and understand the present.

As I have argued throughout this book, journalism in its various avatars has served as a constant link between Spanish America and the question of modernity. A product of the modern age and virtually synonymous with it, journalism has been Spanish American narrative's twin figure, for this is a narrative that has always staked its existence on the search for the modern. Throughout the development of Spanish American narrative fiction, journalism has always been present, fulfilling multiple functions: acting sometimes as a shield for social criticism, sometimes as a foil for aesthetic experimentation or philosophical speculation about the nature of "reality," and often serving as a marker for the broader social and economic contexts that form the background of Spanish American fiction. In this last form, it has acted as the social conscience of Spanish American narrative, helping to keep the focus on extraliterary concerns such as the question of national identity.

Nevertheless, I would stress that journalism has also helped to keep Spanish-American narrative in touch with the basics, not only of its society and culture, but of writing as an activity. As I hope to have made clear, the involvement of Spanish American narrators with journalism has enabled them to reflect on everything from literary techniques to questions of genre, the ideology of authorship, and the ethics of writing. In Chapter 2, we saw how *El Periquillo Sarniento* begins to make strategic use of the blurred borderlines between journalistic and literary discourses. Lizardi's generic dissimulation, which began as an attempt to continue practicing journalism by other means, in the end produced a work that, in a tradition emanating as much from Cervantes as from Lizardi's picaresque models, explored profoundly the complexities of writing and reading. *El Periquillo* is frequently read as a mere description and critique of manners and mores in late-Colonial Mexico, but the stealthy inclusion of journalism in its discourse turns it into a sophisticated writing lesson, a work closer in spirit to the "boom" narratives of the 1960s than to the highly canonized "national romances" of the nineteenth century such as *Amalia* (1851) and *María* (1867).[24] Arguably, *El Periquillo*'s inquiry into dissimulation, disguises, and masks in the context of Mexican society prefigures a highly productive thematic vein of Mexican literature found in twentieth-century writers as diverse as Rodolfo Usigli, Salvador Elizondo, Carlos Fuentes, and Octavio Paz.

If the power of a literary work is to be judged by its capacity to provoke polemics, glosses, and imitations well beyond its epoch, then Sarmiento's *Facundo* must be regarded as one of Spanish American literature's few real powerhouses, a work that still produces passionate debate among its readers. In my analysis in Chapter 3, I showed how at least some of *Facundo*'s fecundity is due to Sarmiento's use of the discourses of sensationalist journalism and the crime story to structure his narrative. Like Lizardi, Sarmiento wrote on the fuzzy edges of the journalism–literature divide, but with a different intention: Lizardi needed to camouflage his pamphlets as novels to escape censorship, Sarmiento sought to give his journalistic attacks against the Rosas dictatorship a broad appeal by couching them in the melodramatic rhetoric of sensationalist journalism. Another contrast between the works is that Lizardi wrote *El Peri-*

quillo to escape the censor's vigilance, whereas Sarmiento's *Facundo* aims to institute a subversive "counter-vigilance" to that of the dictator. Sarmiento sought to endow *Facundo* with journalism's apparent powers of *panoptic* scrutiny, its seeming capacity to simultaneously survey places near and far and to expose what is hidden. Not the least of *Facundo*'s paradoxes is the fact that this journalistic power and authority that the text aims to acquire is based on the same principle of *super-vision* used by the dictator Rosas. In Sarmiento we see, more clearly than in Lizardi, the beginnings of an ethical dilemma that has deeply troubled Spanish American writers in more recent times: the apparent collusion between narrative and authoritarianism.

More sensitive to the authoritarian tendency present in such narrative works as novels and history books, the Peruvian Ricardo Palma used journalistic discourse to subvert it. As I showed in Chapter 4, in his *Tradiciones peruanas* Palma adopts the modes of satirical journalism and the *fait-divers* to create a new, sui generis narrative form, the *tradición*. These brief texts published in newspapers all over the South American continent, give a critical account of Peruvian history, one that not only resists being pigeonholed into a generic category (neither short story, nor essay on manners, nor historical essay, nor autobiography, etc.) but which undermines the solemn genealogical foundations of nineteenth-century historiography, a historiography used by the Peruvian ruling class to legitimize its power. By looking in his *Tradiciones* at the gossipy, human, and fallible side of the supposedly monumental events and personages of the past, Palma rewrites Peruvian history "journalistically," thus depriving it of its foundational character.

Palma's questioning of the idea of "historical origin" and his implicit search for a new beginning from which to launch a modernizing agenda made him into one of the few Spanish American Romantics whom the turn-of-the-century Modernists viewed sympathetically. With the Modernists, the rather free and easy (and sometimes strategic, as already mentioned) give-and-take between journalistic and literary discourses that had been the norm in Spanish America entered into a crisis. Intent on modernizing Spanish American literature, Modernists such as Martí, Nájera, and Darío looked first to journalism as a possible resource. After all, virtually all the turn-of-the-century writers in Spanish America ended up working for the ever more powerful dailies, such as Argentina's *La Nación,* Chile's *El Mercurio,* and Mexico's *El Partido Liberal.* Such work, besides giving them a relatively large measure of financial independence, had increased their professional self-awareness and their pride in being exclusively writers (not lawyers, politicians, or landowners who happened to write, as their Romantic predecessors had been). But journalism, though it taught the Modernists much about the historicity and the material constraints of writing, also questioned profoundly the transcendental notions of selfhood and authority the Modernists had learned from Romantic philology. In their quest to modernize Spanish American literature, the Modernists had taken as their model the turn-of-the-century European search for "art for art's sake," but their experience in journalism (particularly the writing of the brief, descriptive articles they called *crónicas*) had challenged their belief in the autonomy, dignity, and value of literature in society. The Modernists, however, resisted journalism's implicit devaluation of their most cherished ideals, and it fell to a subsequent generation of writers, that of the avant-garde, to come to grips with this ideological impasse.

The Spanish American avant-gardists, exemplified by Borges, broke through this impasse by imitating in their works numerous traits of the journalistic discourse of their time (the demotion of the author, the spatialization of language, the penchant for brevity and synthesis, a certain frivolity). This imitation had the effect of neutralizing journalism's claims to be fundamentally different from fiction. The avant-gardists showed that journalism's claims of empirical veracity were spurious and that rhetorically there is little to distinguish journalistic discourse from that of narrative fiction.

The epistemological prestige – so to speak – of journalism was decisively undermined by the avant-gardists, with the result that in much of contemporary Spanish American narrative fiction the press is no longer portrayed as an emblem of modernity or an agent of modernization. Nevertheless, journalism recurs in numerous contemporary Spanish American literary works. This recurrence seems to follow a consistent pattern, one in which journalism helps to focus implicit ethical or moral reflections. As I have argued in this chapter, journalism's close historical relationship to political and economic power led many of its practitioners to reflect on the ethical aspects of their profession; these reflections help articulate in today's Spanish American narratives what I have called an "ethics of writing," an insistent questioning of the entanglements of narrative (be it fictional or otherwise) with the sources of power and authority in society. By using journalism as a metaphor for ethical reflection about writing, such contemporary authors as García Márquez, Vargas Llosa, and Poniatowska undermine the authoritarian tendencies inherent in the act of narration and involve readers in the production of their literary works, opening up the still-elitist concept of literature in Spanish America to the values of democracy and pluralism.

Notes

All translations of quoted material are by the author, except where noted otherwise.

1 Journalism, modernity, and narrative fiction in Spanish America

1 Two accounts by on-the-spot observers are Harrison Salisbury's *Tiananmen Diary* and Lee Feigon's *China Rising: The Meaning of Tiananmen*. A discussion of journalism and modernization in the Chinese context is found in Jeffrey C. Kinkley, "Modernism and Journalism in the Works of Chang Hsin-hsin."

2 The bibliography on modernity is too vast to summarize here. Along with Matei Calinescu's *Five Faces of Modernity*, my understanding of the concept owes much to Marshall Berman's insightful work, *All That Is Solid Melts Into Air*.

3 By far the most theoretically sophisticated discussion of the paradox of modernity in Spanish America is found in the first chapter of Carlos J. Alonso's *The Spanish American Regional Novel: Modernity and Autochtony*. Other important and recent sources on the topic are such books as Octavio Paz's broad-ranging *Children of the Mire*, Angel
Rama's *Rubén Darío y el modernismo*, Noé Jitrik's *Las contradicciones del modernismo*, and such essays as Roberto González Echevarría's "Modernidad, modernismo, y nueva narrativa," and José Joaquín Brunner's "Entonces, ¿Existe o no la modernidad en América Latina?"

4 The classic reference in this regard is still Stanley and Barbara Stein's *The Colonial Heritage of Spanish America: Essays on Economic Dependence in Perspective*.

5 A lucid analysis of the Cuban situation is found in volume 1 of Manuel Moreno Fraginals' *El ingenio: Complejo económico–social cubano del azúcar*.

6 The fundamentally rhetorical nature of the civilization/barbarism opposition is discussed in Carlos J. Alonso, "Civilización y barbarie."

7 Mitchell Stephens quotes the Englishman John Bell, owner of the *Oracle and Public Advertiser*, who in the spring of 1794 went to Flanders to witness firsthand the fight between the English allies and the French. Unable to secure correspondents there for his

newspaper, Bell declared: "I shall be my own Journalist" (Stephens, p. 237).

8 The bibliography on the literature–journalism problematic in Europe and the United States is abundant and diverse, although it tends more toward description than toward analysis and theory. The following is a brief selection of those texts I have found particularly useful or relevant to my research; many contain additional relevant bibliography. With regard to the eighteenth and nineteenth centuries in England, see Robert Altick, *Deadly Encounters: Two Victorian Sensations;* Jeremy Black, *The English Press in the Eighteenth Century;* Lennard Davis, *Factual Fictions: The Origins of the English Novel;* Paul J. Hunter, "'News and New Things': Contemporaneity and the Early English Novel;" and Ian Watt, *The Rise of the Novel.* On French literature, see Jean-Louis Bory, "Premiers éléments pour une esthétique du roman-feuilleton;" Daniel Compère, "Une écriture romanesque: Le reportage;" Jacques Lethève, *Impressionnistes et symbolistes devant la presse;* and Henri Mitterand, *Zola journaliste de l'affaire Manet à l'affaire Dreyfus.* Regarding the United States, the bibliography is especially rich, particularly on topics such as the "nonfiction novel" and the "new journalism." A broad-ranging study (that also offers useful bibliographic information) is Shelley Fisher Fishkin's *From Fact to Fiction: Journalism and Imaginative Writing in America.* On the "nonfiction novel" and the "new journalism," see: Barbara Foley, *Telling the Truth: The Theory and Practice of Documentary Fiction;* Mas'ud Zavarzadeh, *The Mythopoeic Reality: The Postwar American Nonfiction Novel;* and John Hellman, *Fables of Fact.* In Spain, two compendious works by María Cruz Seoane offer valuable information on the historical interactions between journalism, literature, and oratory in the Peninsula: *Historia del periodismo en España: II: El siglo XIX,* and *Oratoria y periodismo en la España del siglo XIX.* Juan Ignacio Ferreras studies the related phenomenon of the serial novel in Spain in *La novela por entregas, 1840–1900 (Concentración obrera y economía editorial).* There are some general studies on the literature–journalism link available in Spanish and Portuguese: José Acosta Montoro's rather rambling and anecdotal two-volume text, *Periodismo y literatura,* Mario Castro Arenas' excessively brief and schematic *El periodismo y la novela contemporánea,* and, though also brief, by far the most insightful of the three, Alceu Amoroso Lima's *O jornalismo como gênero literário.*
There is also a large body of writing by journalism scholars on the nature of journalistic discourse: works such as Michael Schudson's *Discovering the News: A Social History of American Newspapers,* Gaye Tuchman's *Making News: A Study in the Construction of Reality,* and Herbert J. Gans's *Deciding What's News: A Study of CBS Evening News, NBC Nightly News, Newsweek and Time.* Although these and other works tend to be highly empiricist and anecdotal (and al-

most always focused on the U.S. media), they offer interesting glimpses into the practical realities of journalism. Further bibliography on this topic is found in Fisher and in Mitchell Stephens, *A History of News: From the Drum to the Satellite.*

9 Of all the major Spanish American authors, Gabriel García Márquez has most frequently been studied in relation to his work as a journalist. Some useful essays on this topic are: Aníbal González, "The Ends of the Text: Journalism in the Fiction of Gabriel García Márquez;" Ellen Williamson Kanervo, "Gabriel García Márquez: Journalist as Novelist, Novelist as Journalist;" Robert N. Pierce, "Fact or Fiction? The Developmental Journalism of Gabriel García Márquez;" Robert L. Sims, "El laboratorio periodístico de Gabriel García Márquez: Lo carnavalesco y la creación del espacio novelístico;" Raymond L. Williams, "An Introduction to the Early Journalism of García Márquez: 1948–1958;" and Randolph Pope, "Transparency and Illusion in García Márquez's *Chronicle of a Death Foretold.*" Texts on other contemporary authors such as Carpentier, Cortázar, Donoso, Lezama Lima, and Barnet include María del Carmen Cerezo, "Donoso y los artículos de *Ercilla;*" Roberto González Echevarría, "Carpentier, crítico de la literatura hispanoamericana: Asturias y Borges" (on Carpentier's literary journalism), and *"Biografía de un cimarrón* and the novel of the Cuban Revolution" (on Miguel Barnet's documentary fiction); V. A. Smith, "Carpentier's Journalism in Relation to His Works of Fiction;" Carmen Vásquez, "Alejo Carpentier: Historien de son époque;" Myrna Solotorevsky, "Paradojas e incumplimientos en *Libro de Manuel,*" and José Prats Sariol, "Lezama Lima, periodista." On the journalism of the Spanish-American Modernists, see Aníbal González, *La crónica modernista hispanoamericana.* Some recent essays on the journalism of specific Modernists such as Martí, Silva, and Lugones are: Jorge Marbán, "Evolución y formas en la prosa periodística de José Martí;" Kessel Schwartz, "A Source for Three Martí Letters: The Art of Translation and Journalistic Creation;" Enrique Santos Molano, "José Asunción Silva, el periodista desconocido;" and Gwen Kirkpatrick, "Art and Politics in Lugones' Early Journalism." Books and essays of a general nature on literature, journalism, and society in Spanish America, include Angel Rama, *La ciudad letrada;* Alvaro Barros-Lemez, "Ciudad, prensa y literatura en el 900 rioplatense;" Luis Gregorich, "Literatura: una descripción del campo: Narrativa, periodismo, ideología" (focuses on Argentina); Francine Masiello, "Argentine Literary Journalism: The Production of a Critical Discourse;" Martin S. Stabb, "The New Essay of Mexico: Text and Context;" and Lois Parkinson Zamora, "Novels and Newspapers in the Americas."

10 Literature's dubious institutional nature is probably linked to the aforementioned difficulty in defining it as a type of discourse. I am still persuaded by Foucault's memorable formulation: "Litera-

ture is the contestation of philology (of which it is nevertheless the twin figure): it leads language back from grammar to the naked power of speech, and there it encounters the untamed, imperious being of words. From the Romantic revolt against a discourse frozen in its own ritual pomp, to the Mallarméan discovery of the word in its impotent power, it becomes clear what the function of literature was, in the nineteenth century, in relation to the modern mode of being of language. Against the background of this essential interaction, the rest is merely effect: literature becomes progressively more differentiated from the discourse of ideas and encloses itself within a radical intransitivity; it becomes detached from all the values that were able to keep it in general circulation during the Classical age (taste, pleasure, naturalness, truth) and creates within its own space everything that will ensure a ludic denial of them (the scandalous, the ugly, the impossible); it breaks with the whole definition of genres as forms adapted to an order of representations and becomes merely a manifestation of a language that has no other law than that of affirming – in opposition to all other forms of discourse – its own precipitous existence; and so there is nothing for it to do but curve back in perpetual return upon itself, as if its discourse could have no other content than the expression of its own form; it addresses itself to itself as a writing subjectivity, or seeks to re-apprehend the essence of all literature in the movement that brought it into being; and thus all its threads converge upon the finest of points – singular, instantaneous and yet absolutely universal – upon the simple act of writing" (*Les mots et les choses*, p. 313).

11 Among "the oldest direct ancestors of the newspaper" are the gazettes published in Venice in the mid-sixteenth century (Stephens, p. 152), which gathered political or military information for the benefit of merchants and diplomats. The notion of the bourgeois origins of the novel and the short story is already a critical commonplace.

12 An excellent introduction to the promising as well as controversial effects of chaos theory on literary analysis and critical theory is found in Hayles (ed.), *Chaos and Order: Complex Dynamics in Literature and Science*. The essays in that collection explore, among other issues, the validity of using scientific models – no matter how nondeterministic in appearance – in literary criticism. To some, the use of chaos theory in a literary context might look like a covert attempt to bring back positivistic notions such as the "science of literature." I am persuaded, however, that chaos theory, along with relativity and Heisenberg's Uncertainty Principle in quantum mechanics, has essentially given the coup de grace to positivism in contemporary scientific discourse. However, one might question the need to use chaos as a source of tropes in literary analysis (Hayles, p. 20), since critical theory already pro-

vides a rich analytical terminology in modes such as deconstruction. Nevertheless, although deconstruction works in a fashion similar to chaos theory (in its suspicion of totalization, the importance it assigns to levels of scale, and its emphasis on iterative and recursive techniques; Hayles, p. 11), it does so either at a discrete, intratextual level, or on a broader philosophical and intertextual plane. In order to speak about the relationship between two discourses such as literature and journalism, I need a terminology that allows me to describe textual phenomena which occur at an intermediate scale: neither altogether intratextually nor altogether intertextually. The lexicon of chaos theory fits the bill by allowing me to visualize the interaction of these two discourses dynamically, in a fluid manner, rather than as a mere question of frames or borders. Or, to put it in another way, chaos theory allows me to see the border between literature and journalism as a fractal entity, that is, as a design of constantly repeated patterns on different scales (see Gleick, pp. 98–103).

13 Stephens, pp. 13–20. A cogent and condensed analysis of the fundamentals of narrative may be found in Hayden White's "The Value of Narrativity in the Representation of Reality."

14 Although prefaces and manifestos should always be taken with a grain of salt, abundant evidence of the realists' reluctance to critique journalism and of their affinity with journalistic discourse is found in several of these documents, such as George Eliot's preface to *Adam Bede* (1859), the Goncourts' preface to *Germinie Lacerteux* (1865), and Zola's manifestolike essay, "Le roman expérimental" (1880). See Becker (ed.), *Documents of Modern Literary Realism*.

15 This struggle was mostly ideological and political, of course, and was also waged in other areas of life by writers who belonged to the various social classes, but additionally it was, I would argue, a textual struggle for self-definition in both the journalistic and the fictional realms. As I have already stated, in my view Western literature (of which Spanish American literature forms a part) has developed within a field of competing discourses, one that does not merely reflect the competition between social classes and interest groups in society, but is also a struggle among discourses for self-foundation and institutional recognition. I derive these ideas mainly from Foucault, but to a certain extent my understanding of the mode of existence of discourses in society also resembles the one outlined by British communications theorist Stuart Hall and his associates at the Centre for Contemporary Cultural Studies at the University of Birmingham. See Hall's essays "Encoding/Decoding" and "Recent Developments in Theories of Language and Ideology: A Critical Note," as well as Dave Morley's "Text, readers, subjects," in *Culture, Media, Language*. I also owe a substantial debt to Edward Said's Foucauldian study of how the West

has reconceptualized the East, as a discourse and as a discipline, in *Orientalism.*

16 There are surprisingly few comprehensive overviews of the history of Spanish American journalism. The most easy to find is probably Andrés Henestroza and José Antonio Fernández de Castro's brief work, *Periodismo y periodistas de Hispanoamérica* (1947), originally published in 1941 as an appendix to the Spanish translation of Georges Weill's general history of journalism, *Le Journal: origines, evolution et rôle de la presse periodique* (1934). A more voluminous, equally reliable, but more obscure work is *La cultura y el periodismo en América* (1953) by Gustavo Adolfo Otero. Otero appears to have been unaware of Weill's and Henestroza's works.

17 See Henestroza and Fernández de Castro, pp. 45–50; Otero, pp. 295–309, 467–77; also Antonio S. Pedreira, *El periodismo en Puerto Rico*, pp. 33–191; Federico Alvarez O., *Labor periodística de Don Andrés Bello;* Arturo Fontaine Aldunate, "Andrés Bello, formador de opinión pública;" and Carlos García Barrón, "El periodismo peruano del siglo XIX."

18 In his book *Imagined Communities: Reflections on the Origins and Spread of Nationalism*, Benedict Anderson argues that the concept of nationhood in the Americas is inseparably linked to the rise of the newspapers (pp. 61, 65). Although I believe he is essentially correct, I feel Anderson overemphasizes the importance of the print media in the process of nation-building. Furthermore, in discussing journalistic discourse, he is too quick to presuppose its fictive nature ("reading a newspaper is like reading a novel whose author has abandoned any thought of a coherent plot," p. 33n). In my own approach, I consider it more fruitful to problemize the question of journalism's relation to fictional discourse. Anderson's sources for his statements about journalism in the Americas also strike me as distressingly meager: He does not cite any specific book or article on the subject, relying instead, apparently, on John Lynch's historical work, *The Spanish American Revolutions, 1808–1826*, and Jean Franco's *An Introduction to Spanish American Literature*. Additionally, his admission in the "Preface to the Second Edition" of his work that he was unable to read Spanish when he wrote his book renders suspect his commentary on works such as Lizardi's *El Periquillo Sarniento* (*Imagined Communities*, pp. 29–32).

19 Otero states: "This period of the press in the Americas may be regarded as the golden moment of journalism of opinion. . . . The importance of journalism as an instrument to lead and interpret public opinion reaches its apogee, and it is then that journalism is designated as the Fourth Estate [*el Cuarto Poder del Estado*]" (p. 156).

20 In *O jornalismo como gênero literário*, Alceu Amoroso Lima remarks that as the cinema and the electronic mass media have risen in importance in the last few decades, written journalism has increas-

ingly become a literary genre of sorts, and the distance between journalism and literature has grown correspondingly smaller (pp. 9–10).

2 *Journalism and (dis)simulation in* El Periquillo Sarniento

1 By far the most up-to-date scholarly work on *El Periquillo Sarniento* has been done by Nancy Vogeley, in her unpublished dissertation "*El Periquillo Sarniento:* The Problem of Mexican Independence" (1980) and in several recent essays. Vogeley follows in the footsteps of Mexican and U.S. scholars who have produced erudite and interpretative work on *El Periquillo* since the turn of the century: from Luis González Obregón to Jefferson Rea Spell, Alfonso Reyes, Agustín Yáñez, and many others. I have relied a good deal, for contextual and erudite questions, on Vogeley's scrupulous work, although my interpretation of *El Periquillo* moves in a quite different direction from her socioliterary view. For instance, whereas she takes note of Lizardi's "mimicry," she discusses it only in the context of the concept of "colonial discourse" as defined by Homi Bahba (see Vogeley, "Defining the 'Colonial Reader'").

Analogous discriminations apply to my approach vis-à-vis a recent essay on Lizardi by Jean Franco, "La heterogeneidad peligrosa: Escritura y control social en vísperas de la independencia mexicana." Where Franco views Lizardi as a mere spokesman for an incipient "bourgeois ideology" in independence-era Mexico, I tend to see his texts in a more problematic light. I am also wary of positing links between *El Periquillo* and a particular ideology, in view of the difficulties involved in identifying and defining specific ideologies in early nineteenth-century Mexico and of the difficulties in *reading* Lizardi's novel thoroughly and accurately.

2 This in spite of the fact (to which critics always allude with irritation) that the text is heavily interlaced with lengthy moral digressions of a patently oratorical nature. Although most critics today recognize such digressions as an integral part of this text, there is still a tendency to read around them, rather than through them. Unable to discard them outright as mere residues of Lizardi's journalistic inclinations, critics have attempted to relate these passages to the rest of the text on the basis of *El Periquillo*'s avowed links to the picaresque genre, in particular to such equally digressive and moralistic works as Mateo Alemán's *Guzmán de Alfarache* (1605). Nevertheless, such attempts simply defer the question of what these passages signify in Lizardi's text.

3 For further details, see Spell, *Bridging the Gap*, pp. 121, 145.

4 For a detailed catalogue of Lizardi's sources, see Spell, *Bridging the Gap*, pp. 149–70.

5 The title of the English translation of this novel is *The Itching Parrot*. Aside from leaving out the diminutive, this translation, like

my own, prefers the more generic adjective "itching" to the more precise though less poetic "mangy" for "sarniento."

6 This view of the orient as an empty stage in which the European fantasies of individual self-fashioning and freedom from societal constraints took place was to become even more prevalent in the Romantics, as can be seen in the travel-narratives of Lane, Chateaubriand, Lamartine, Nerval, and Flaubert. See Said, pp. 149–97.

7 "If we were to meet an allegorical character in real life, we would say of him that he was obsessed with only one idea, or that he had an absolutely one-track mind, or that his life was patterned according to absolutely rigid habits from which he never allowed himself to vary. It would seem that he was driven by some hidden, private force; or, viewing him from another angle, it would appear that he did not control his own destiny, but appeared to be controlled by some foreign force, something outside the sphere of his own ego" (Fletcher, pp. 40–1).

8 Possible sources for Lizardi are Iriarte's *Fábulas literarias* (1780), and, going further back in time, Sebastián de Covarrubias Orozco's *Emblemas morales* (1610). In "Emblema 78" of the "Centuria I," Covarrubias presents the drawing of a caged parrot with the Latin words *Refert dictata* emblazoned above it; the accompanying poem in *ottava rima* and its gloss in prose chastise preachers and teachers who memorize other people's texts without understanding them and then recite them as their own. Spell points out in *El Periquillo*'s text a quotation from the *Empresas políticas* of Saavedra Fajardo (Spell, *Bridging the Gap*, p. 168). More recent elaborations upon the symbol of the parrot all derive from Flaubert, and may be found in such contemporary novels as Julian Barnes' *Flaubert's Parrot* (1984), Gabriel García Márquez's *Love in the Time of Cholera* (1985), and Mario Vargas Llosa's *The Storyteller* (1987).

9 I am following Derrida's well-known reading of Rousseau in *Of Grammatology*, pp. 141–64.

10 *El Periquillo* is full of scenes of "sensibility," in which both men and women display an extreme tenderness and spontaneous feelings of compassion toward others. Sentimental fiction may be seen as the dramatization of a polemic between two influential views of human nature in the eighteenth century: Hobbes' and Smith's view (in *Leviathan* [1651] and *The Wealth of Nations* [1776], respectively) of humanity as irremediably sinful, egotistical, and power-driven, and that of Shaftesbury and Hume, for whom humans have an intrinsic moral sense that produces in them a natural tendency toward benevolence, philanthropy, and social harmony. In eighteenth-century sentimental narratives (from Richardson and Sterne to Rousseau and Goethe) the struggle between these two visions of human nature is presented as a clash between a

benevolent, virtuous, and sensitive protagonist (in the mold of Shaftesbury and Hume) and an egotistic, ruthless, and utilitarian society as envisioned by Hobbes and Smith (Janet Todd, *Sensibility: An Introduction*). Although Periquillo is a rogue who seems to be innately disposed only toward imitation, the text insists on presenting him as a naive, credulous soul, who would easily behave virtuously when pushed in the right direction. Don Antonio (who is himself the protagonist of an episode of sensibility) says as much when he reencounters the reformed Periquillo after many years:

> Ever since I met that young man, I was persuaded that his crimes were due more to his imitation of his evil friends than from any malignity of his character. . . . I saw that . . . Periquillo was evil because of the urgings of his evil friends rather than from a heart full of malice, and I was convinced that, once he was rid of those provocative enemies, he would by himself be well-disposed towards virtue. (p. 444)

11 Periquillo quotes some of *El Pensador*'s disclaimers to those who praise his work: "Gentlemen, do not be fooled; I am not wise, educated, nor erudite. I realize how much one needs to know in order to fulfill such titles. My writings dazzle you when you read them for the first time, but they are nothing but tinsel. I myself am ashamed to see mistakes printed which I did not notice when I wrote them. The ease with which I write is no evidence of talent" (p. 454).

12 In the "Prólogo, dedicatoria y advertencias a los lectores," Lizardi dedicates *El Periquillo* to his readers (rather than to any nobleman or bourgeois), stating that they are his true patrons and masters (pp. 3–4). A passage from one of Lizardi's pamphlets (number 11, Volume I of *El Pensador Mexicano* [1813]) prefigures the link between Lizardi as a journalist and the *pícaro*: "The most violent winding-frame in all its movement does not cartwheel more than my own thoughts about all things imaginable. And since my thought is so light and is not bound to times nor places, it goes jumping from kingdom to kingdom, from epoch to epoch and from century to century. In this manner, I as soon become a statesman as a general; sometimes I am a doctor, others a priest; sometimes an artisan, a farmer, a merchant, a sailor, a soldier, and finally a *Petrus in cunctis*, a meddler and a gossip (but about vices, not about people)" (*Obras. III*, p. 97). This statement may be fruitfully contrasted to similar ones made by the Mexican Modernist Manuel Gutiérrez Nájera, at the end of the nineteenth century, about the journalist's protean nature (see Chapter 5): while Lizardi exults in his diversity of *personae* and his powers of transformation, Nájera deplores journalism's undermining of the writer's identity and authority.

3 Sarmiento and sensationalist journalism

1 The view of Oedipus as a proto-detective, which seems an obvious one, has been propounded by such German scholars as Wolgang Schadewalt, "Der *König Oedipus* des Sophokles in neuer Deutung" (1956); Ernst Bloch, "Philosophische Ansicht des Detektivromans" (1960; cited, along with Schadewalt, in Reinert, p. 7), and Claus Reinert, *Detektivliteratur bei Sophokles, Schiller und Kleist, oder Das Rätsel der Wahrheit und die Abenteuer des Erkennens* (1975). Such a notion has not been popular, however, with scholars who attempt some sort of definition or "poetics" of the crime story. Ernest Mandel, for example, states that a major difference between crime as it appears in Sophocles and in detective fiction is that in the latter it is "reified" and deprived of a "preoccupation with human destiny" (p. 41). In a similar vein, John G. Cawelti points out that, in contrast to a detective story, in *Oedipus Rex* "detection leads to a revelation of hidden guilts in the life of the protagonist, while in the detective story the inquirer-protagonist and the hidden guilt are conveniently split into two separate characters – the detective and the criminal – thereby enabling us to imagine terrible crimes without also having to recognize our own impulses toward them" (in Winks, p. 134; see also Grossvogel, pp. 23–4, 39–40, and, from the perspective of "narratology," Todorov, pp. 42–52). Such objections seem to hinge, at bottom, on the anachronism of calling Oedipus a "detective," and do not dispute the fact that Sophocles' character was a solver of mysteries, including crime. Robin Winks remarks that "the ideal detective story is the one in which the detective hero discovers that he (or she) is the criminal. The implicit psychological assumption there is markedly modern, but it rests upon the oldest definitions of mystery as 'a hidden or inexplicable matter.' Oedipus, *The Moonstone*, William Hjorstberg's *Falling Angel* (1978) are a continuing stream by which one penetrates 'what is common in human experience through time'" (p. 5).

2 Mandel (pp. 1–19), Murch (pp. 18–66), and Symons (pp. 17–53), among others, coincide in classing crime ballads, crime journalism, the *feuilleton*, and the "Newgate novel," as early examples of the crime story. On the Spanish crime ballads, see Caro Baroja. On the "Newgate novel," see Hollingsworth.

3 The biography of celebrated outlaws was a common topic of the popular Spanish *literatura de cordel*, a genre Sarmiento probably knew firsthand. See "Acciones y prosas bárbaras (Bandolerismo)" in Caro Baroja, pp. 349–405.

4 Stephens attributes to Bennett the introduction of "on-the-spot reporting" (pp. 242–4) and the idea of the press not merely as "the Jury of the Nation," but as an active agent in "ferreting out crime, and aiding to bring criminals to justice" (Bennett, cited by Stephens, p. 245).

5 According to Dottori and Zanetti, historians currently give little credence to Sarmiento's thesis of Rosas' complicity in the murder of Facundo (Sarmiento, p. 15, note 13).

6 See Roberto González Echevarría's detailed analysis of this passage, "Redescubrimiento," pp. 401–6.

7 "The gestures of life call forth a series of interrogations aimed at discovering the meanings implicit in them. The narrative voice is not content to describe and record gesture, to see it simply as a figure in the interplay of persons with one another. Rather, the narrator applies pressure to the gesture, pressure through interrogation, through the evocation of more and more fantastic possibilities, to make it yield meaning, to make it give up to consciousness its full potential as 'parable'" (Brooks, p. 1). Might this semantic "pressure" Brooks identifies in the rhetoric of melodrama not be related to the rhetorical "pressure exerted upon the readers" of *Facundo*, seen by Jitrik (p. 11)? I disagree with Garrels in her interpretation of Sarmiento's overall attitude toward melodrama and of two well-known melodramatic episodes in Chapters 10 and 12 of *Facundo* (both of which I analyze below). She argues that Sarmiento was ambivalent toward the excesses of melodrama, and cites various highly ironic theater reviews Sarmiento wrote of Gothic plays, such as "La nona sangrienta," as well as passages from *Facundo*, in support of her observation (pp. 438–40). Nevertheless, although it is understandable that Sarmiento, whose educational propensities are well-known, would not totally approve of melodrama in the theater, he was clearly not immune to its attractiveness as a rhetorical device. Melodrama is furthermore not merely a form of entertainment (as Garrels seems to believe, p. 440) but, as Brooks convincingly argues, of interpretation: it is a Manichaean, antithetical way of viewing ideas and the world, and in this sense melodrama is profoundly linked to the main thesis of Sarmiento's book.

8 In this regard, see Alonso's "Facundo y la sabiduría del poder."

9 Sarmiento's comments immediately following his typology of the gaucho are ambiguously suggestive of the diversity of his self-dramatization in the text: "In the course of this story, the reader shall discover for himself where the tracker, the scout, the outlaw, or the singer may be found" (p. 50). On the role of "voice" and orality in *Facundo*, see Ramos.

4 Journalism versus genealogy

1 An originator of this attitude was William Wordsworth, about whom M. H. Abrams has observed that he "did not merely level the Neoclassic order, but turned it upside down, by preferring in his subjects the last over the first and by transforming the humble and the passive into the heroic, the low into the sublime, and the

petty into the numinous. Hence . . . the extraordinary protagonists, for example, of his serious and tragic narratives, who speak
and are described in a language replete with biblical overtones –
not demigods, kings, noblemen, warriors, or even members of the
middle classes, nor only peasants, pedlars and wagoners, but also
the ignominious, the disinherited, the criminal, and the outcast;
superannuated soldiers, beggars, convicts, murderers, abandoned
mothers, infanticides, holy idiots, and stoical leech-gatherers
threatened with technological unemployment, who move through
his poems with a sacramental dignity and unknowingly exert a
charismatic power" (*Natural Supernaturalism*, pp. 396–7).

2 See G. S. Rousseau, *Organic Form: The Life of an Idea.*

3 Letter to Pastor Obligado. Quoted by Oviedo, pp. xxviii–xxix.

4 For example: "My style is exclusively mine, very mine. So much so
that it has placed me in the same situation as the hunchback who
put on a mask to attend a Carnival ball. His hunchback gave him
away. And my form and style in prose cannot be so disagreeable,
when I have found in America so many writers who follow the
school I founded. . . . For me, a *tradición* is not a light piece of
work, but a work of art. I smooth and polish my phrases with a
Benedictine's patience. It is their form, more than their content,
that has made them so popular" (Letter to Vicente Barrantes, in
Ricardo Palma, *Epistolario*, p. 334).

5 Ricardo Palma, *Tradiciones peruanas completas*, pp. 500–12, 795–9.
All quotes are from this edition.

6 For example: "In 1851, the poet Trinidad Fernández and I, an
eighteen-year-old youngster, were chroniclers and proofreaders
in *El Correo de Lima*, a daily that had replaced *El Correo Peruano*,
with the substantial salary of thirty pesos per month. What a bar-
gain!" (p. 1122).

7 I have developed this interpretation of the essay on manners in my
book *La crónica modernista hispanoamericana*, pp. 65–70. See also the
classic study by Margarita Ucelay Da Cal, *Los españoles pintados por
sí mismos (1843–1844): Estudio de un género costumbrista.*

8 A good summary of the diversity of critical approaches to satire is
found in *Satire: Modern Essays in Criticism*, ed. Ronald Paulson.

9 Edward W. Rosenheim, Jr., defines satire as "an attack by means of
a manifest fiction upon discernible historic particulars," and
points out that when those "historic particulars" cease to be recognized as such by the readers, the satire becomes ineffective. "The
Satiric Spectrum," in Paulson, pp. 323 and passim.

10 White, *Metahistory*, p. 263. I also follow here the ideas of Roland
Barthes in "Le discours de l'histoire."

11 In his discussion of causal agents in allegories, Angus Fletcher
points out that "the term 'daemonic' was reserved for devils only
by a late and naïve tradition; the more liberal view gave to
daemons an intermediate position and maintained precisely the

present view of the kosmoi, that like them the agents can be either above or below mankind. The effect of meeting an allegorical agent is to be raised (by an angel) or lowered (by a devil), but in no case to be unaffected with respect of the rank of the daemon" (p. 120). For her part, Margarita Ucelay Da Cal, in her description of the picaresque tradition of the "diablo cojuelo" in the essay on manners, explains that Asmodée (the French writers' name for the "diablo cojuelo") represents "the abstract idea of a spirit that uncovers and reveals the wickedness, foolishness, and weaknesses covered by hypocrisy in peoples' lives, by the conventions of social behavior" (p. 88). A more general discussion of the "Metamorphoses of Satan" in romantic literature can be found in Mario Praz's classic *La carne, la morte e il diavolo nella letteratura romantica.*

12 Regarding the romantic transvaluation of the Devil as a figure of authority, see, besides Praz's book, M. H. Abrams, *The Mirror and the Lamp: Romantic Theory and the Critical Tradition,* pp. 250–6.

13 Edith Palma's edition redeems itself, however, by including a "Serial Index" of the *Tradiciones peruanas.*

14 Discussing Nietzsche's use of the term *Ursprung* in *The Genealogy of Morals,* Michel Foucault wonders: "Why does Nietzsche challenge the pursuit of the origin (*Ursprung*), at least on those occasions when he is truly a genealogist? First, because it is an attempt to capture the exact essence of things, their purest possibilities, and their carefully protected identities, because this search assumes the existence of immobile forms that precede the external world of accident and succession. This search is directed to 'that which was already there,' the image of a primordial truth fully adequate to its nature, and it necessitates the removal of every mask to ultimately disclose an original entity. However, if the genealogist refuses to extend his faith in metaphysics, if he listens to history, he finds that there is 'something altogether different' behind things: not a timeless and essential secret, but the secret that they have no essence or that their essence was fabricated in a piecemeal fashion from alien forms" ("Nietzsche, Genealogy, History," in *Language, Counter-Memory, Practice,* p. 142). Does this same movement to question origins and genealogies *by means of* historical evocation not occur in the *Tradiciones peruanas?* What else does Palma discover when he goes back to the origins of Peruvian history but a multiplicity of origins that dissolve into the murmurings of gossip, folk sayings, and old wives' tales? If a biographical explanation for Palma's antigenealogical impulse were sought, perhaps it might be found in his humble personal origins. Julio Díaz Falconí alludes to Palma's "African blood" and observes: "It is surprising that a man so given to revealing confidential information never revealed the name of his mother." ("Palma, personaje de sí mismo," in Flores, *Orígenes del cuento hispanoamericano,* p. 52.) It is certain, however, that it was Palma's journalistic apprenticeship

that gave him the instruments to carry out his disconcerting enterprise.

15 Ricardo Palma, "Prólogo" to Clorinda Matto de Turner, *Tradiciones cuzqueñas,* pp. ix–x.

16 "In 1881 the author had written most of a long historical novel titled *Los marañones,* whose manuscript disappeared in the fire of Miraflores." Note in Ricardo Palma, *Tradiciones peruanas completas,* p. 75.

17 The fact that, in his old age, "with the idea of ingratiating himself with certain powerful men," Palma partially abandoned his critical project, as Julio Díaz Falconí points out (Flores, p. 53), does not invalidate the essentially subversive and modernizing effect of Palma's oeuvre. This was noted by Rubén Darío when he associated Palma, in his article "Fotograbado" (1890), with the "new spirit" of "*modernismo*": "He [Palma] is decidedly affiliated with classical decorum, and he respects the Academy. But he understands and admires the new spirit that today moves a small but triumphant and proud group of writers and poets of Spanish America: modernism" (quoted by Max Henríquez Ureña, *Breve historia del modernismo,* pp. 158–9).

5 Journalism and the self

1 In *Rubén Darío y el modernismo (Circunstancia socioeconómica de un arte americano),* Angel Rama remarked on this, adding that, for the Modernists, "poetry and journalism were intermixed in their daily work, going unceasingly from one to the other, in the same day, over the same writing-desk" (p. 76). I have explored further the Modernists' dependence on journalism to publish their works as well as to earn their daily bread in my book *La crónica modernista hispanoamericana.* As I argue in these pages, journalism was responsible to a very great extent for the Modernists' "modernity."

2 On Carpentier, see Roberto González Echevarría's essay, "Modernidad, modernismo, y nueva narrativa: *El recurso del método.*" For a more extensive overview of the newer critical works in which Modernism is reevaluated, see my book *La novela modernista hispanoamericana,* pp. 17–19; also *La crónica modernista hispanoamericana,* pp. 8–12.

3 See Schulman's *Génesis del modernismo: Martí, Gutiérrez Nájera, Silva, Casal* and his essay "Reflexiones en torno a la definición del modernismo," p. 329.

4 A more detailed development of this idea is found in *La crónica modernista hispanoamericana,* pp. 5–59, 75–6.

5 See the introduction to Nájera's *Obras. Crítica literaria,* p. 65.

6 Quoted by Boyd G. Carter in his "Estudio preliminar" to Nájera's *Divagaciones y fantasías. Crónicas de Manuel Gutiérrez Nájera,* p. 14.

7 Andrés Iduarte, *Martí escritor,* pp. 133–6. The fact that Martí

wrote his articles for *The Sun* and *The Hour* in French is revealed in an intriguing note by Alejo Carpentier in his book *Chroniques*, in which he remarks: "But the person who contributed most decisively to make Flaubert's work known to the Spanish-speaking public was, without a doubt, the great Cuban critic, poet, and patriot, José Martí (1853–1895), whom we regard as the most universal thinker of nineteenth-century Latin America. . . . Flaubert died on 8 May 1880, leaving unfinished the manuscript of *Bouvard et Pécuchet*, which would not appear in book form until the following year, after its publication had been announced for the month of December in the *Revue nouvelle* of Mme. Aubin. . . . Now then, on 8 July 1880, exactly two months after Flaubert's death, José Martí, who lived in New York at the time, published in the daily *The Sun* a long essay about *Bouvard et Pécuchet* in which he emphasized the remarkable and unique nature of this novel. . . . From where did Martí get his information? It is a total mystery. His article in *The Sun* – written in French, since he did not have on hand a good translator from Spanish into English – is evidence of the amazing diffusion of Flaubert's work in the Hispanic world" (pp. 494–5).

8 Flaubert's two best-known statements in this regard are found in his *Correspondance*, III, pp. 37, 61.

9 I have examined this chronicle in greater detail in *La crónica modernista hispanoamericana*, pp. 84–97.

10 For an excellent discussion of the epistemology of the museum in a literary context, see Eugenio Donato's essay "The Museum's Furnace: Notes Towards a Contextual Reading of *Bouvard and Pécuchet*."

11 Quoted by Manuel Pedro González and Ivan A. Schulman in *José Martí, Esquema ideológico*, p. 63.

12 For the full list, see E. K. Mapes, "Manuel Gutiérrez Nájera. Seudónimos y bibliografía periodística."

13 The best of the very few overall assessments of Gómez Carrillo is John W. Kronik's "Enrique Gómez Carrillo, Francophile Propagandist."

14 On the impact of photography and film on the rise of the artistic avant-garde, see Shattuck, pp. 223–51, and Poggioli, pp. 175–206.

15 See Vitier's essay, "Martí futuro," in Vitier and García, *Temas martianos*, pp. 120–39. Also González Echevarría's "Martí y su 'Amor de ciudad grande': Notas hacia una poética de los *Versos libres*."

6 *Journalism and the ethics of writing*

1 Although he takes a jaundiced view of this particular manifestation of avant-garde experimentalism, Renato Poggioli summarizes its development thus: "Starting from the theory of *typographical emphasis*, dear to Mallarmé in his later phase and to the futurists,

which gave a page of poetry the guise of a poster or a musical score, Apollinaire added to it what he called *visible lyricism:* a graphic-figurative correspondence between the manuscript or printed poem and the sense or imagery of that poem" (Poggioli, pp. 133–4). For a more sympathetic view of avant-garde attempts to blur the borderlines between the various art forms, see Bürger, pp. 47–54. Pérez-Firmat notes the importance of the palimpsest as an emblem of writing in the Hispanic Vanguardist novels. In novels such as Jaime Torres Bodet's *Margarita de niebla* (1927), Pérez-Firmat points out, "the very idea of depth is called into question. This procedure seems to demonstrate that depth is nothing more than an illusion created by the multiplication of surfaces. In probing deeper and deeper [the character] Borja replicates images, but he never abandons the realm of the superficial or the epidermic, since beneath the surface there lie only other surfaces. Depth thus appears as an *effect* of rigorously superficial superpositions. Another way of putting this is to say that Borja perceives Margarita as a palimpsest, an object which furnishes us with an exact textual correlate of Borja's corridor of receding mirrors" (p. 94; italics in original).

2 See Carlos J. Alonso's convincing analyses of *Doña Bárbara, La vorágine,* and *Don Segundo Sombra* in his book *The Spanish American Regional Novel: Modernity and Autochthony.*

3 See Roberto González Echevarría's pertinent comments on one of Carpentier's most journalistic – and most autobiographical – novels, *Los pasos perdidos* (*The Lost Steps,* 1953), in *Alejo Carpentier: The Pilgrim at Home,* pp. 162–189.

4 Conversation with the distinguished Peruvian novelist, Alfredo Bryce Echenique, who has himself participated in the "Grandes Firmas" series and is a frequent collaborator in Spanish and Spanish American newspapers such as *El País* (Madrid), *El Sol* (Madrid), *ABC* (Madrid), and *El Comercio* (Lima); Madrid, June 30, 1991.

5 With regard to the United States, Hulteng reproduces the full texts of the Canons of the American Society of Newspaper Editors (ASNE, adopted in 1922) and the Code of Ethics of the Society of Professional Journalists, Sigma Delta Chi, adopted in 1973 (pp. 18–24). Basically, these codes deal with the behavior of journalists in their daily work and with the content of newspapers, according to such categories as "Responsibility," "Freedom of the Press," "Independence," "Accuracy and Objectivity," "Impartiality," "Fair Play," and "Decency." But Hulteng also cautions that these codes "cannot be compared with legal or medical codes, since in those fields ethical principles are enforced by licensing agencies and policing bodies. It is also the case that the medical and legal codes are more specific and rigid than those that have been developed in the field of journalism" (p. 229). Latin America's Sociedad Interamericana de Prensa (Inter-American Press Association [IAPA]),

of which the United States is also a member, and whose origins date to the First Panamerican Congress of Journalists held in Washington, D.C., in 1926, has always been more preoccupied with issues of press freedom and government censorship in its member countries than with the everyday ethical questions addressed by the ASNE and Sigma Delta Chi codes. Despite well-known unethical practices in Latin American journalism, such as the *iguala* system in Mexico and news pirating by radio stations from the print media (as seen in Vargas Llosa's *Aunt Julia and the Scriptwriter*), the IAPA has never adopted a uniform code of ethics, although several have been proposed at various times. A detailed account of these attempts, and the ethical issues that had been raised in the IAPA's history before 1960, is found in Gardner, *The Inter-American Press Association: Its Fight for Freedom of the Press, 1926–1960* (pp. 38–48). A historical study of the development of standards of journalistic conduct in the U.S., which serves to give some idea of the ethical complexities in which journalism has always been immersed, is Dicken-García's *Journalistic Standards in Nineteenth-Century America.* See also Goodwin, *Groping for Ethics in Journalism.*

6 Sometimes characters explicitly connected with the church would fulfill an ethical function in the narrative, as in Periquillo's numerous encounters with priests and his final submission to Christian morality in the Casa Profesa (Lizardi, *El Periquillo Sarniento*, Chapter 9), or in the Modernist Manuel Gutiérrez Nájera's playfully devout alter ego, "El Duque Job," during his "Cuaresmas" ("Lenten Sermons;" Henríquez Ureña, pp. 70–1).

7 This "ethics of writing" would be complementary to the one posited by J. Hillis Miller in *The Ethics of Reading*, a book from which I have profited much.

8 See González, "The Ends of the Text," and, for a slightly different perspective, Parkinson Zamora, "Ends and Endings."

9 For further details on allusions to journalism in these works, see González, "The Ends of the Text," pp. 63–6.

10 García Márquez's comments about journalism and its impact on his work, in published interviews such as Plinio Apuleyo Mendoza's *El olor de la guayaba*, are not very useful in this regard, since they remain concerned with the purely practical level of literary technique (González, "The Ends of the Text", pp. 63, 67–8). It is in his fiction that a deeper, though implicit, meditation is to be found.

11 See the perceptive comments by González Echevarría in his note, "Big Mama's Wake."

12 I am alluding to Derrida's usage of the term "dissemination": an operation performed by certain texts that consists of making meaning circulate indefinitely through several different domains (science, mathematics, philosophy, etc.) until the boundaries that define meaning are erased (see Derrida's *Dissemination*).

13 Barthes, *Critical Essays*, pp. 190–2.

14 I have traced some of these links in detail in "The Ends of the Text"; among them are the allusions to the story of Christ's crucifixion encoded in many of the characters' names and roles, the onomastic double-entendres and allusions to literary tradition in such names as "Vicario" and "María Alejandrina Cervantes," and such episodes as the one about the stray bullet that smashed the plaster saint and the one in which Santiago disguises María Alejandrina's mulatto girls, mixing up their identities (*Chronicle of a Death Foretold*, pp. 12, 87–8). See "The Ends of the Text," pp. 68–71. See also Alonso, "Writing and Ritual in *Chronicle of a Death Foretold*."

15 See Borges, "Una vindicación del falso Basílides," in *Discusión*, pp. 61–6. The French philosopher of science Michel Serres has written extensively on the relationship between "background noise" and the origin of the text in *Hermès IV: La Distribution* as well as in *Le Parasite*.

16 Jonathan Culler comments on this in "The Uses of *Madame Bovary*," in *Flaubert and Postmodernism*, pp. 1–12.

17 In this context, Vargas Llosa's lukewarm review of Sartre's voluminous study of Flaubert, *L'Idiot de la famille* 1971–2), is highly illuminating. Like other critics, Vargas Llosa declares *L'Idiot de la famille* to be "an extraordinarily uneven book" ("Flaubert, Sartre y la nueva novela," p. 221). More revealing, however, are Vargas Llosa's autobiographical comments in this article tracing his reactions to the changing appreciation of Flaubert by French intellectuals of the fifties and sixties, as well as his final, rather bizarre equivalence of Flaubert and Sartre, when he asks rhetorically: "Can there be a greater resemblance, a failure that is just as admirable, and for the same reasons, as that between *L'Idiot de la famille* and *Bouvard et Pécuchet*?" ("Flaubert, Sartre y la nueva novela," p. 223). Vargas Llosa also trenchantly emphasizes the moral importance of Sartre to his work: "Sartre is one of the authors to whom I believe I owe the most, and at one time I admired his writings almost as much as those of Flaubert. Through the years, however, his creative work has been fading in my memory, and his statements about literature and the writer's role, which once I regarded as unquestionable, now no longer seem so convincing. . . . His moral figure, in contrast, looms ever larger for me, in the crises and dilemmas of these difficult years, because of the lucidity, honesty, and bravery with which he has faced not only fascism, conservatism, and the traps of the bourgeoisie, but also authoritarianism and the quasi-religious fanaticism of the left" (p. 220). A lucid exposition of Sartre's literary ideas is found in Halpern, *Critical Fictions: The Literary Criticism of Jean-Paul Sartre*.

18 Whether the text of *Aunt Julia and the Scriptwriter* actually exemplifies such a balance is debatable. See Alonso's remarks in "*La tía*

Julia y el escribidor: The Writing Subject's Fantasy of Empowerment," p. 57, n5.

19 To dramatize the difficulties inherent in defining this genre, Lucille Kerr catalogues the variety of terms that critics and authors
alike have applied to it: from "documentary fiction" to "novela-
testimonio" (p. 370, n. 1). In this chapter, I use the terms "documentary fiction," "documentary novel," and "documentary narrative" interchangeably, mostly to avoid repetition. I nevertheless
ask the reader to bear in mind Kerr's *caveat:* "Different terms
means different things to different readers; different texts elicit
different labels from different quarters" (p. 370, n. 1).

20 The roster of works of Spanish American documentary fiction
grows every year, but a number of authors have already achieved
importance within this genre: Along with Poniatowska, primacy
certainly belongs to the Cuban Miguel Barnet, whose entire narrative production after *The Autobiography of a Runaway Slave* consists
of documentary fictions: *Canción de Rachel* ("Rachel's Song,"
1969), *Gallego* ("Gallego," 1981), and *La vida real* ("Real Life,"
1989), among others. Recent critical bibliography on documentary
fiction may be found in Kerr, pp. 393–4.

21 The "Cretan Liar" paradox is also known simply as "the Liar Paradox," and it is one of the most famous and ancient of logical
paradoxes. An engaging account is found in Falletta, *The Paradoxicon*, pp. 75–86.

22 This is true of works with a clearly accusatory intent, such as
Massacre in Mexico, Rodolfo Walsh's *Operación masacre* (*Operation
Massacre*, 1957), Jacobo Timerman's *Prisionero sin nombre, celda sin
número* (*Prisoner Without a Name, Cell Without a Number*, 1980), and
Antonio Skármeta's *Soñé que la nieve ardía* (*I Dreamed the Snow was
Burning*, 1975). It is true as well as of those that appear to be either
more dispassionate, such as Barnet's *The Autobiography of a Runa-
way Slave* and García Márquez's *The Story of a Shipwrecked Sailor*, or
more frivolous, such as Barnet's *Canción de Rachel*, Edgardo
Rodríguez Juliá's *El entierro de Cortijo* ("Cortijo's Burial," 1983), or
Umberto Valverde's *Celia Cruz: Reina Rumba* ("Celia Cruz: Queen
Rhumba," 1981). On Rodríguez Juliá, see González's review essay,
"Edgardo Rodríguez Juliá, *El entierro de Cortijo;*" on Valverde, see
Cabrera Infante, "Salsa para una ensalada."

23 See Derrida's reading of this parable by Kafka in *Acts of Literature*.

24 The term "national romances" has been applied to these works by
Doris Sommer in *Foundational Fictions: The National Romances of
Spanish America*.

Bibliography of works cited

Abrams, Meyer H. *The Mirror and the Lamp: Romantic Theory and the Critical Tradition.* New York: Oxford University Press, 1953.
Natural Supernaturalism. Tradition and Revolution in Romantic Literature. New York: W. W. Norton, 1971.

Acosta Montoro, José. *Periodismo y literatura.* 2 vols. Madrid: Editorial Guadarrama, 1973.

Alonso, Carlos, J. "Civilización y barbarie." *Hispania* 72 (May 1989): 256–63.
"Facundo y la sabiduría del poder." *Cuadernos Americanos* 226 (September–October 1979): 116–30.
"*La tía Julia y el escribidor:* The Writing Subject's Fantasy of Empowerment," *PMLA* 106 (1991): 46–59.
The Spanish American Regional Novel: Modernity and Autochthony. Cambridge University Press, 1990.
"Writing and Ritual in *Chronicle of a Death Foretold.*" In *Gabriel García Márquez. New Readings.* Ed. Bernard McGuirk and Richard Cardwell. Cambridge University Press, 1987.

Altick, Robert. *Deadly Encounters: Two Victorian Sensations.* Philadelphia: University of Pennsylvania Press, 1986.

Alvarez, O., Federico. *Labor periodística de Don Andrés Bello.* Caracas: Universidad Central de Venezuela, 1962.

Amoroso Lima, Alceu. *O jornalismo como gênero literário.* Rio de Janeiro: AGIR Editora, 1960.

Anderson, Benedict. *Imagined Communities: Reflections on the Origins and Spread of Nationalism.* London: Verso, 1991.

Arenas, Reynaldo. *El mundo alucinante.* Mexico City: Editorial Diógenes, 1969.

Bakhtin, Mikhail. *Rabelais and His World.* Trans. Hélène Iswolsky. Bloomington: Indiana University Press, 1984.

Barros-Lemez, Alvaro. "Ciudad, prensa y literatura en el 900 ríoplatense." *Revista de Crítica Literaria Latinoamericana* 11 (1985): 137–49.

Barthes, Roland. *Critical Essays.* Trans. Richard Howard. Evanston, Ill.: Northwestern University Press, 1972.
"Le discours de l'histoire." *Social Science Information* (International Science Council) 6 (August 1967): 73–81.

Image/Music/Text. Trans. Richard Howard. New York: Hill and Wang, 1977.

Mythologies. New York: Hill and Wang, 1972.

Bartlett Giamatti, A. "Proteus Unbound: Some Versions of the Sea-God in the Renaissance." In *The Disciplines of Criticism,* ed. Peter Demetz. New Haven: Yale University Press, 1968, pp. 437–76.

Bazin, Robert. *Historia de la literatura americana en lengua española.* Buenos Aires: Editorial Nova, 1958.

Becker, George J., ed. *Documents of Modern Literary Realism.* Princeton: Princeton University Press, 1963.

Bellanger, Claude, Jacques Godechot, Pierre Guiral, and Fernand Terrou, eds. *Histoire générale de la presse française: Tome II: De 1815 à 1871.* Paris: Presses Universitaires de France, 1969.

Bellini, Giuseppe. *Historia de la literatura hispanoamericana.* Madrid: Editorial Castalia, 1985.

Benveniste, Emile. *Problems in General Linguistics.* Trans. Mary Elizabeth Meeks. Coral Gables, Fla.: University of Miami Press, 1971.

Berman, Marshall. *All That Is Solid Melts into Air: The Experience of Modernity.* New York: Penguin, 1989.

Bernucci, Leopoldo M. *Historia de un malentendido: Un estudio transtextual de* La guerra del fin del mundo *de Mario Vargas Llosa.* New York: Peter Lang, 1989.

Black, Jeremy. *The English Press in the Eighteenth Century.* Philadelphia: University of Pennsylvania Press, 1987.

Borges, Jorge Luis. "An Autobiographical Essay." In *The Aleph and Other Stories, 1933–1969.* New York: Dutton, 1970, pp. 203–60.

"Borges y yo." In *El hacedor.* Madrid: Alianza/Emecé, 1972, pp. 69–70.

Borges on Writing. Ed. Norman Thomas Di Giovanni, Daniel Halpern and Frank MacShane. New York: Dutton, 1973.

Discusión. Buenos Aires: Emecé, 1957.

Elogio de la sombra. In *Obra poética.* Madrid: Alianza/Emecé, 1975.

Ficciones. Buenos Aires: Emecé, 1956.

Historia Universal de la Infamia. Madrid: Alianza/Emecé, 1971.

Otras inquisiciones. Buenos Aires: Emecé, 1960.

Bory, Jean-Louis. "Premiers éléments pour une esthétique du roman-feuilleton." In *Musique II: Tout Feu Tout Flamme.* Paris: Juilliard, 1966, pp. 13–41.

Brooks, Peter. *The Melodramatic Imagination: Balzac, Henry James, Melodrama and the Mode of Excess.* New Haven: Yale University Press, 1976.

Brunner, José Joaquín. "Entonces, ¿Existe o no la modernidad en América Latina?" *Punto de Vista* 10 (November–December 1987): 2–5.

Bürger, Peter. *Theory of the Avant-Garde.* Minneapolis: University of Minnesota Press, 1984.

Cabrera Infante, Guillermo. "Salsa para una ensalada." In *Literatures in Transition: The Many Voices of the Caribbean Area.* Ed. Rose S. Minc. Gaithersburg, Md.: Ediciones Hispamérica, 1982, pp. 21–36.

Calinescu, Matei. *Five Faces of Modernity.* Durham: Duke University Press, 1987.

Caro Baroja, Julio. *Ensayo sobre la literatura de cordel.* Madrid: Ediciones de la Revista de Occidente, 1969.

Carpentier, Alejo. *Chroniques.* Paris: Gallimard, 1983.

Casal, Julián del. *Prosas.* Centenary edition, 3 vols. Havana: Consejo Nacional de Cultura, 1963–4.

Castro Arenas, Mario. *El periodismo y la novela contemporánea.* Caracas: Monte Avila, 1969.

Cerezo, María del Carmen. "Donoso y los artículos de *Ercilla.*" *Literatura Chilena: Creación y Crítica* 9 (January–March 1985): 9–11.

Compère, Daniel. "Une écriture romanesque: Le reportage." *Europe: Revue Littéraire Mensuelle* 626–7 (June–July 1981): 38–45.

Cortázar, Julio. *Libro de Manuel.* Buenos Aires: Sudamericana, 1973.

Covarrubias Orozco, Sebastián. *Emblemas morales.* Madrid: n.p., 1610.

Cruz Seoane, María. *Historia del periodismo en España: II: El siglo XIX.* Madrid: Alianza Editorial, 1983.

Oratoria y periodismo en la España del siglo XIX. Madrid: Fundación Juan March y Editorial Castalia, 1977.

Culler, Jonathan. *Flaubert: The Uses of Uncertainty.* Ithaca, N.Y.: Cornell University Press, 1985.

"The Uses of *Madame Bovary.*" In *Flaubert and Postmodernism.* Ed. Naomi Schor and Henry F. Majewski. Lincoln: University of Nebraska Press, 1984, pp. 1–12.

Darío, Rubén. *Obras completas,* 10 vols. Madrid: Afrodisio Aguado, 1950.

Poesías completas. Madrid: Aguilar, 1967.

David, Lennard. *Factual Fictions: The Origins of the English Novel.* New York: Columbia University Press, 1983.

de Man, Paul. *Allegories of Reading: Figural Language in Rousseau, Nietzsche, Rilke, and Proust.* New Haven: Yale University Press, 1979.

Blindness and Insight: Essays in the Rhetoric of Contemporary Criticism. New York: Oxford University Press, 1971.

"Literary History and Literary Modernity." In *Blindness and Insight: Essays in the Rhetoric of Contemporary Criticism.* Minneapolis: University of Minnesota Press, 1983, pp. 142–65.

Derrida, Jacques. *Acts of Literature.* Derek Attridge, ed. New York: Routledge, 1992.

Dissemination. Trans. and with an introduction by Barbara Johnson. Chicago: University of Chicago Press, 1981.

Of Grammatology. Trans. Gayatri Chakravorty Spivak. Baltimore: Johns Hopkins University Press, 1976.

Dicken-García, Hazel. *Journalistic Standards in Nineteenth-Century America.* Madison: University of Wisconsin Press, 1989.

Donato, Eugenio. "The Museum's Furnace: Notes towards a Contextual Reading of *Bouvard and Pécuchet*." In *Textual Strategies: Perspectives in Post-Structuralist Criticism*. Ed. and with an introduction by Josué V. Harari. Ithaca, N.Y.: Cornell University Press, 1979, pp. 213–38.

Escobar, Alberto. *Patio de letras*. Lima: Ediciones Caballo de Troya, 1965.

Falleta, Nicholas L. *The Paradoxicon*. New York: Doubleday, 1983.

Feigon, Lee. *China Rising: The Meaning of Tiananmen*. New York: Ivan R. Dee, 1990.

Fernández de Lizardi, José Joaquín. *El Periquillo Sarniento*. Mexico City: Porrúa, 1970.

    The Itching Parrot. Trans. Eugene Pressly; ed. Katherine Anne Porter. Garden City, N.Y.: Doubleday, 1942.

    Obras. I. Poesías y fábulas. Ed. Jacobo Checinsky and Luis Mario Schneider. Mexico City: UNAM, 1963.

    Obras, III: Periódicos: El Pensador Mexicano. Ed. María Rosa Palazón and Jacobo Checinsky; Prologue by Jacobo Chencinsky. Mexico City: UNAM, 1968.

    Obras, IV: Periódicos. Ed. María Rosa Palazón. Mexico City: UNAM, 1970.

Ferreras, Juan Ignacio. *La novela por entregas, 1840–1900 (Concentración obrera y economía editorial)*. Madrid: Taurus, 1972.

Fisher Fishkin, Shelley. *From Fact to Fiction: Journalism and Imaginative Writing in America*. New York: Oxford University Press, 1985.

Flaubert, Gustave. *Correspondance*. 9 vols. Paris: Conard, 1926–33.

    "A Simple Heart." In *Three Tales*. Trans. Robert Baldick. London: Penguin, 1961, pp. 17–56.

Fletcher, Angus. *Allegory: The Theory of a Symbolic Mode*. Ithaca, N.Y.: Cornell University Press, 1964.

Flores, Angel, ed. *Orígenes del cuento hispanoamericano (Ricardo Palma y sus tradiciones)*. Mexico City: Premiá, 1979.

Foley, Barbara. *Telling the Truth: The Theory and Practice of Documentary Fiction*. Ithaca, N.Y.: Cornell University Press, 1986.

Fontaine Aldunate, Arturo. "Andrés Bello, formador de opinión pública." *Atenea: Revista de Ciencia, Arte y Literatura de la Universidad de Concepción* 443–4 (1981): 117–34.

Foster, David William. "Latin American Documentary Narrative." *PMLA* 99 (1984): 41–55.

Foucault, Michel. *Histoire de la folie à l'âge classique*. Paris: Gallimard, 1972.

    Language, Counter-Memory, Practice. Ed. Donald F. Bouchard. Ithaca, N.Y.: Cornell University Press, 1977.

    Les mots et les choses. Paris: Gallimard, 1966.

    L'Ordre du discours. Paris: Gallimard, 1971.

    The Order of Things: An Archeology of the Human Sciences. New York: Pantheon, 1970.

Franco, Jean. "La heterogeneidad peligrosa: Escritura y control social en vísperas de la independencia mexicana." *Hispamérica* 12 (1983): 3–34.

Gans, Herbert J. *Deciding What's News: A Study of CBS Evening News, NBC Nightly News, Newsweek and Time.* New York: Pantheon, 1979.

García Barrón, Carlos. "El periodismo peruano del siglo XIX." *Cuadernos Hispanoamericanos* 417 (March 1985): 197–204.

García Márquez, Gabriel. *Crónica de una muerte anunciada.* Bogotá: Oveja Negra, 1981.

Los funerales de la Mamá Grande. Xalapa, Mex.: Universidad Veracruzana, 1962.

El olor de la guayaba. Interviews with Plinio Apuleyo Mendoza. Bogotá: Oveja Negra, 1982.

Gardner, Mary A. *The Inter-American Press Association: Its Fight for Freedom of the Press, 1926–1960.* Austin: University of Texas Press, 1967.

Garrels, Elizabeth. "El *Facundo* como folletín." *Revista Iberoamericana* 143 (April–June 1988): 419–48.

Gleick, James. *Chaos: Making a New Science.* New York: Penguin, 1988.

Gómez Carrillo, Enrique. *El primer libro de las crónicas.* Madrid: Mundo Latino, 1919.

González, Aníbal. "Edgardo Rodríguez Juliá, *El entierro de Cortijo.*" *Sin Nombre* 13 (1983): 82–6.

La crónica modernista hispanoamericana. Madrid: Porrúa Turanzas, 1983.

"The Ends of the Text: Journalism in the Fiction of Gabriel García Márquez." In *Gabriel García Márquez and the Power of Fiction,* ed. Julio Ortega. Austin: University of Texas Press, 1988.

La novela modernista hispanoamericana. Madrid: Gredos, 1987.

González Echevarría, Roberto. *Alejo Carpentier: The Pilgrim at Home.* Austin: University of Texas Press, 1990.

"Big Mama's Wake." *Diacritics* (1974): 55–8.

"*Biografía de un cimarrón* and the Novel of the Cuban Revolution." In *The Voice of the Masters.* Austin: University of Texas Press, 1985.

"Carpentier, crítico de la literature hispanoamericana: Asturias y Borges." In *Isla a su vuelo fugitiva: Ensayos críticos sobre literatura hispanoamericana.* Madrid: Porrúa Turanzas, 1983, pp. 179–204.

"Martí y su 'Amor de ciudad grande': Notas hacia una poética de los *Versos libres.*" In *Isla a su vuelo fugitiva: Ensayos críticos sobre literatura hispanoamericana.* Madrid: Porrúa Turanzas, 1983, pp. 27–42.

"Modernidad, modernismo, y nueva narrative: *El recurso del método.*" *Revista Interamericana de Bibliografía/Inter-American Review of Bibliography* 30 (1980): 157–63.

Myth and Archive: A Theory of Latin American Narrative. Cambridge University Press, 1991.

"Redescubrimiento del mundo perdido: El *Facundo* de Sarmiento." *Revista Iberoamericana* 143 (April–June 1988): 385–406.

Goodwin, Eugene. *Groping for Ethics in Journalism.* Ames: Iowa University Press, 1983.

Gould, Stephen Jay. *Bully for Brontosaurus: Reflections in Natural History.* New York: Norton, 1991.

Gregoritch, Luis. "Literatura: Una descripción del campo: Narrativa, periodismo, ideología" in *Represión y reconstrucción de una cultura: El caso argentino.* Ed. Saúl Sosnowski. Buenos Aires: Universidad de Buenos Aires, 1988, pp. 109–24.

Grossvogel, David I. *Mystery and Its Fictions: From Oedipus to Agatha Christie.* Baltimore: Johns Hopkins University Press, 1979.

Gutiérrez Nájera, Manuel. *Divagaciones y fantasías: Crónicas de Manuel Gutiérrez Nájera.* Ed. and with an introduction by Boyd G. Carter. Mexico City: Secretaría de Educación Pública, 1944.

Escritos inéditos de sabor satírico, "*Plato del día.*" Ed. and with an introduction by Boyd G. Carter; notes by Mary Eileen Carter. Columbia: University of Missouri Press, 1972.

Obras: Crítica literaria. Collected by E. K. Mapes. Ed. and with notes by Ernesto Mejía Sánchez; introduction by Porfirio Martínez Peñaloza. Mexico City: Universidad Nacional Autónoma, 1959.

Hall, Stuart, Dorothy Hobson, Andrew Lowe, and Paul Willis, eds., *Culture, Media, Language.* London: Hutchinson, Centre for Contemporary Cultural Studies, 1980.

Halpern, Joseph, *Critical Fictions. The Literary Criticism of Jean-Paul Sartre.* New Haven: Yale University Press, 1976.

Hayles, N. Catherine. "Introduction: Complex Dynamics in Literature and Science." In *Chaos and Order: Complex Dynamics in Literature and Science.* Chicago: University of Chicago Press, 1991, pp. 1–36.

Hellman, John. *Fables of Fact.* Urbana: University of Illinois Press, 1981.

Henestroza, Andrés, and José Antonio Fernández de Castro. *Periodismo y periodistas de Hispanoamérica.* Mexico City: Secretaría de Educación Pública, 1947.

Henríquez Ureña, Max. *Breve historia del modernismo.* Mexico City: Fondo de Cultura Económica, 1954.

Henríquez Ureña, Pedro. *Las corrientes literarias en la América Hispánica.* Mexico City: Fondo de Cultura Económica, 1978 [1949].

Historia de la cultura en la América Hispánica. Mexico City: Fondo de Cultura Económica, 1975.

Hollingsworth, Keith. *The Newgate Novel.* Detroit: Wayne State University Press, 1963.

Hulteng, John L. *The Messenger's Motives: Ethical Problems of the News Media.* Englewood Cliffs, N.J.: Prentice-Hall, 1976.

Hunter, Paul J. "'News and New Things': Contemporaneity and the Early English Novel." *Critical Inquiry* 14 (Spring 1988): 493–515.

Iduarte, Andrés. *Martí escritor.* Havana: Ministerio de Educación, Dirección de Cultura, 1951.

Iriarte, Tomás de. *Fábulas literarias.* Islas Canarias: Biblioteca Básica Canaria, 1989.

Jitrik, Noé. *Las contradicciones del modernismo.* Mexico City: El Colegio de México, 1978.

—— *Muerte y resurrección del Facundo.* Buenos Aires: Centro Editor de América Latina, 1983.

Joyce, James. *Ulysses.* New York: Vintage, 1961.

Kanervo, Ellen Williamson. "Gabriel García Márquez: Journalist as Novelist, Novelist as Journalist." *Midwest Quarterly: A Journal of Contemporary Thought* 26 (Summer 1985): 467–75.

Kant, Immanuel. *Immanuel Kants Werke.* Vol. 5. Ed. Ernst Cassirer. Berlin: Bruno Cassirer, 1912–1918.

Kernan, Alvin B. "The Idea of Literature." *New Literary History* 1 (1973): 31–40.

Kerr, Lucille. "Gestures of Authorship: Lying to Tell the Truth in Elena Poniatowska's *Hasta no verte Jesús mío.*" *MLN* 106 (1991): 370–94.

Kinkley, Jeffrey C. "Modernism and Journalism in the Works of Chang Hsin-hsin." *Tamkang Review: A Quarterly of Comparative Studies between Chinese and Foreign Literatures* 18 (Autumn 1987–Summer 1988): 97–123.

Kirkpatrick, Gwen. "Art and Politics in Lugones' Early Journalism" *Discurso Literario* 3 (1985): 81–95.

Kronik, John W. "Enrique Gómez Carrillo, Francophile Propagandist." *Symposium* 21 (1967): 50–60.

Lafforgue, Jorge, "Mario Vargas Llosa: Moralista." In *Nueva novela latinoamericana.* Buenos Aires: Paidós, 1969, pp. 209–40.

Larousse Encyclopedia of Mythology. New York: Prometheus Press, 1959.

Lethève, Jacques. *Impressionnistes et symbolistes devant la presse.* Paris: Presses Universitaires de France, 1959.

Mandel, Ernest. *Delightful Murder: A Social History of the Crime Story.* London: Pluto Press, 1984.

Mapes, E. K. "Manuel Gutiérrez Nájera: Seudónimos y bibliografía periodística." *Revista Hispánica Moderna* 1–4 (1953): 132–204.

Marbán, Jorge. "Evolución y formas en la prosa periodística de José Martí." *Revista Iberoamericana* 55 (January–June 1989): 211–22.

Mariátegui, José Carlos. *Seven Interpretive Essays on Peruvian Reality.* Trans. Marjory Urquidi. Introduction by Jorge Basadre. Austin: University of Texas Press, 1971.

Martí, José. *Esquema ideológico.* Collected and with introductions by Manuel Pedro González and Ivan A. Schulman. Mexico City: Editorial Cultura, 1961.

—— *Obras completas.* Vol. 7. Havana: Editorial Nacional de Cuba, 1963.

Masiello, Francine. "Argentine Literary Journalism: The Production of a Critical Discourse." *Latin American Research Review* 20 (1985): 27–60.

Merrim, Stephanie. "For a New (Psychological) Novel in the Works of Manuel Puig." *Novel* 17 (1984): 141–57.

Miller, D. A. *The Novel and the Police*. Berkeley: University of California Press, 1988.

Miller, J. Hillis. *The Ethics of Reading: Kant, de Man, Eliot, Trollope, James and Benjamin*. New York: Columbia University Press, 1987.

Miró Quesada Laos, Carlos. *Historia del periodismo peruano*. Lima: Librería Internacional del Perú, 1957.

Mitterand, Henri. *Zola journaliste de l'affaire Manet à l'affaire Dreyfus*. Paris: Presses Universitaires de France, 1962.

Moreno Fraginals, Manuel. *El ingenio: Complejo económico–social cubano del azúcar*. 3 vols. Havana: Editorial de Ciencias Sociales, 1978.

Murch, Alma Elizabeth. *The Development of the Detective Novel*. New York: Philosophical Library, 1958.

Nietzsche, Friedrich. *Das Philosophenbuch: Theoretische Studien*. Paris: Aubier-Flammarion, 1969.

Ortega y Gasset, José. *La deshumanización del arte y otros ensayos de estética*. Madrid: Ediciones de la Revista de Occidente, 1976.

Otero, Gustavo Adolfo. *La cultura y el periodismo en América*. Quito: Casa Editora Liebmann, 1953.

Oviedo, José Miguel. *Mario Vargas Llosa: La invención de una realidad*. Barcelona: Seix Barral, 1982.

"Palma entre ayer y hoy." Prologue to Ricardo Palma, *Cien tradiciones peruanas*. Caracas: Biblioteca Ayacucho, 1977, pp. ix–xli.

Palma, Angélica. *Ricardo Palma*. Buenos Aires: Editorial Tor, 1933.

Palma, Ricardo. *Epistolario*. Lima: Editorial Cultura Antártica, 1949.
"Prólogo." In Clorinda Matto de Turner, *Tradiciones cuzqueñas*. Cuzco: n.p., 1954, pp. ix–x.
Tradiciones peruanas completas. Ed. and with a prologue by Edith Palma. Madrid: Aguilar, 1953.

Parkinson Zamora, Lois. "Ends and Endings in García Márquez's *Crónica de una muerte anunciada*." *Latin American Literary Review* 13 (1985): 104–16.
"Novels and Newspapers in the Americas." *Novel: A Forum on Fiction* (forthcoming).

Paulson, Ronald, ed. *Satire: Modern Essays in Criticism*. Englewood Cliffs, N.J.: Prentice-Hall, 1971.

Paz, Octavio. *Children of the Mire: Modern Poetry from Romanticism to the Avant-Garde*. Trans. Rachel Phillips. Cambridge, MA: Harvard University Press, 1974.

Pedreira, Antonio S. *El periodismo en Puerto Rico*. Río Piedras: Editorial Edil, 1982.

Pérez-Firmat, Gustavo. *Idle Fictions: The Hispanic Vanguard Novel, 1926–1934*. Durham, N.C.: Duke University Press, 1982.

Philp, Mark, "Michel Foucault." In *The Return of Grand Theory in the*

Human Sciences. Ed. Quentin Skinner. Cambridge University Press, 1985, pp. 65–82.

Pierce, Robert N. "Fact or Fiction? The Developmental Journalism of Gabriel García Márquez." *Journal of Popular Culture* 22 (Summer 1988): 63–71.

Poggioli, Renato. *The Theory of the Avant-Garde.* Cambridge, Mass.: Harvard University Press, 1968.

Poniatowska, Elena. *Hasta no verte, Jesús mío.* Mexico City: Ediciones Era, 1969.

La noche de Tlatelolco. Mexico City: Ediciones Era, 1971.

Pope, Randolph. "Transparency and Illusion in García Márquez' *Chronicle of a Death Foretold.*" *Latin American Literary Review* 15 (January–June 1987): 183–200.

Prats Sariol, José. "Lezama Lima, periodista." *Plural: Revista Cultural de Excelsior*, 18 (April 1989): 69–72.

Praz, Mario. *La carne, la morte e il diavolo nella letteratura romantica.* Florence: G. C. Sansoni, 1950.

Quesada y Miranda, Gonzalo de. *Martí, periodista.* Havana: Imprenta y Papelería de Rambla, Bouza y Co., 1929.

Rama, Angel. *La ciudad letrada.* Hanover, N.H.: Ediciones del Norte, 1984.

Rubén Darío y el modernismo. Caracas: Biblioteca de la Universidad Central de Venezuela, 1970.

Ramos, Julio. "Escritura y oralidad en el *Facundo.*" *Revista Iberoamericana* 143 (April–June 1988): 551–69.

Reinert, Claus. *Detektivliteratur bei Sophokles, Schiller und Kleist, oder Das Rätsel der Wahrheit und die Abenteuer des Erkennens.* Kronberg: Scriptor Verlag, 1975.

Renan, Ernest. *L'Avenir de la science: Pensées de 1848.* Paris: Calmann-Lévy, 1890.

Rodó, José Enrique. "Cómo ha de ser un diario." In *Obras completas.* Madrid: Aguilar, 1967, pp. 1198–201.

Rojas y Cañas, Ramón. "Porquerías y adefesios." In *Costumbristas y satíricos de Terralla a Yerovi, I.* Ed. Ventura García Calderón. Paris: Desclée de Brower, 1938, pp. 268–75.

Rousseau, G. S. *Organic Form: The Life of an Idea.* London: Routledge & Kegan Paul, 1972.

Said, Edward. *Orientalism.* New York: Vintage, 1979.

Salisbury, Harrison. *Tiananmen Diary.* New York: Little, Brown, 1990.

Santos Molano, Enrique. "José Asunción Silva, el periodista desconocido." *Boletín Cultural y Bibliográfico* 18 (1981): 79–86.

Sarduy, Severo. *La simulación.* Caracas: Monte Avila, 1982.

Sarmiento, Domingo Faustino. *Facundo, o Civilización y Barbarie.* Prologue by Noé Jitrik; notes and chronology by Nora Dottori and Silvia Zanetti. Caracas: Biblioteca Ayacucho, 1977.

Schudson, Michael. *Discovering the News: A Social History of American Newspapers.* New York: Basic Books, 1978.

Schulman, Ivan A. *Génesis del modernismo: Martí, Gutiérrez Nájera, Silva, Casal.* Mexico City: Colegio de México, 1966.

"Reflexiones en torno a la definición del modernismo." In *Estudios críticos sobre el modernismo.* Ed. Homero Castillo. Madrid: Gredos, 1968.

Schwartz, Kessel. "A Source for Three Martí Letters: The Art of Translation and Journalistic Creation." *Revista de Estudios Hispánicos* 18 (January 1984); 133–53.

Serres, Michel, *Hermès IV: La Distribution.* Paris: Minuit, 1977.

Le Parasite. Paris: Grasset, 1980.

Shattuck, Roger. *The Banquet Years: The Origins of the Avant-Garde in France: 1885 to World War I.* New York: Vintage, 1968.

Silva Castro, Raúl. *Prensa y periodismo en Chile (1812–1956).* Santiago: Ediciones de la Universidad de Chile, 1958.

Sims, Robert L. "El laboratorio periodístico de Gabriel García Márquez: Lo carnavalesco y la creación del espacio novelístico." *Revista Iberoamericana* 52 (October 1986): 979–89.

Smith, V. A. "Carpentier's Journalism in Relation to His Works of Fiction." *Crítica Hispánica* 7 (1985): 159–74.

Solotorevsky, Myrna. "Paradojas e incumplimientos en *Libro de Manuel.*" *Hispamérica,* 15 (August 1986): 19–28.

Spell, Jefferson Rea. *Bridging the Gap: Articles on Mexican Literature.* Mexico City: Editorial Libros de México, 1971.

Sommer, Doris. *Foundational Fictions: The National Romances of Latin America.* Berkeley: University of California Press, 1991.

Stabb, Martin S. "The New Essay of Mexico: Text and Context." *Hispania* 70 (March 1987): 47–61.

Stein, Stanley and Barbara. *The Colonial Heritage of Spanish America: Essays on Economic Dependence in Perspective.* New York: Oxford University Press, 1970.

Stephens, Mitchell. *A History of News: From the Drum to the Satellite.* New York: Viking, 1988.

Symons, Julian. *Bloody Murder: From the Detective Story to the Crime Novel: A History.* Harmondsworth: Viking, 1985.

Todd, Janet, *Sensibility: An Introduction.* London: Methuen, 1986.

Todorov, Tzvetan. *The Poetics of Prose.* Trans. from the French by Richard Howard. Ithaca: Cornell University Press, 1977.

Tuchman, Gaye. *Making News: A Study in the Construction of Reality.* New York: Free Press, 1978.

Ucelay Da Cal, Margarita. *Los españoles pintados por sí mismos (1843–1844): Estudio de un género costumbrista.* Mexico City: Colegio de México, 1951.

Vargas Llosa, Mario. "Flaubert, Sartre y la nueva novela." In *Contra viento y marea (1962–1982).* Barcelona: Seix Barral, 1983, pp. 216–24.

La guerra del fin del mundo. Barcelona: Seix Barral, 1981.

La tía Julia y el escribidor. Barcelona: Seix Barral, 1971.

La verdad de las mentiras. Barcelona: Seix Barral, 1990.

A Writer's Reality. Syracuse, N.Y.: Syracuse University Press, 1991.

Vásquez, Carmen. "Alejo Carpentier: Historien de son époque" in *Alejo Carpentier et son oeuvre.* Paris: Université de Paris-Sorbonne, 1982, pp. 62–74.

Verdevoye, Paul. *Domingo Faustino Sarmiento: Educateur et Publiciste (entre 1839 et 1852).* Paris: Institut des Hautes Etudes de l'Amérique Latine, 1963.

Vitier, Cintio, and Fina García Marruz. *Temas martianos.* Río Piedras, Puerto Rico: Editorial Huracán, 1981.

Vogeley, Nancy. "The Concept of 'the People' in *El Periquillo Sarniento.*" *Hispania* 3 (1987): 457–67.

"Defining the 'Colonial Reader': *El Periquillo Sarniento.*" *PMLA* 5 (1987): 784–800.

"Mexican Newspaper Culture on the Eve of Mexican Independence." *Ideologies and Literature* 4.17 (1983): 358–77.

"*El Periquillo Sarniento:* The Problem of Mexican Independence." Unpublished Ph.D. dissertation, Stanford, 1980.

Watt, Ian. *The Rise of the Novel.* Berkeley: University of California Press, 1957.

White, Hayden, *Metahistory: The Historical Imagination in Nineteenth-Century Europe.* Baltimore: Johns Hopkins University Press, 1973.

Tropics of Discourse. Baltimore: Johns Hopkins University Press, 1978.

Williams, Raymond L. "An Introduction to the Early Journalism of García Márquez: 1948–1958." *Latin American Literary Review* 13 (January–June 1985): 117–32.

Winks, Robin, ed. *Detective Fiction: A Collection of Critical Essays.* Woodstock, Vt.: The Countryman Press, 1988.

Wold, Ruth. *El Diario de México, primer cotidiano de Nueva España.* Madrid: Gredos, 1970.

Wordsworth, William. *Wordsworth's Literary Criticism.* Ed. W. J. B. Owen. London: Routledge & Kegan Paul, 1974.

Zavarzadeh, Mas'ud. *The Mythopoeic Reality: The Postwar American Nonfiction Novel.* Urbana: University of Illinois Press, 1976.

Index

Ainsworth, William Harrison, 47
Alamán, Lucas, 4
Alonso, Carlos J., 42
Amalia (José Mármol), 17, 126
Anderson, Benedict, 136n18
Apollinaire, Guillaume, 103
avant-garde, 96, 99, 100, 128–9; and
  journalism, 18, 103–4, 108; key traits
  of, 102–3, 145n1; Ultraist principles,
  103–4

Bakhtin, Mikhail, 69
Balzac, Honoré de, 46, 53, 54, 66, 79,
  81
Barnet, Miguel, 122
Barthes, Roland, 9–10, 63–4, 73–5, 114,
  115
Bazin, Robert, 64
Bello, Andrés, 3, 46, 47
Bennett, James Gordon, 47, 61
Benveniste, Emile, 7
Beyle, Henri (Stendhal), 66
"Big Mama's Funeral" (Gabriel García
  Márquez), 112–13
Bolívar, Simón, 3
"boom" writers, and journalism, 18, 108,
  109–10
Borges, Jorge Luis, 1, 10, 20, 101, 104–
  8, 115, 124, 128
"Borges and I" (Jorge Luis Borges), 101
Bourget, Paul, 98
Brooks, Peter, 52, 53, 54
Bryce Echenique, Alfredo, 146n4
Bulwer-Lytton, Edward, 46, 47

Carpentier, Alejo, 7, 84, 108
Carrió de la Vandera, Alonso, 40
Castellanos, Rosario, 2, 123
Carter, Boyd G., 95
chaos theory, 6, 10–11, 134n12
Columbus, Christopher, 44

Cortázar, Julio, 110
Costumbrismo, 21
crime story: definition of, 47–8; *see also
  Facundo*
*Crónica de una muerte anunciada (Chronicle
  of a Death Foretold;* Gabriel García
  Márquez), 110, 124; and ethics of
  writing, 115–16; *fait-divers* in, 114–15;
  journalism as interpretation in, 113–
  17; and *The War of the End of the
  World,* 120–1
Cruz Seoane, María, 88

da Cunha, Euclides, 120
Dana, Charles, 90
Darío, Rubén, 4, 83, 84, 99, 102, 127
Davis, Lennard, 12, 38–9
de Girardin, Emile, 46
de la Fuente, Modesto (Fray Gerundio),
  67
de Larra, Mariano José, 69
del Casal, Julián, 86–7, 88, 89, 102
de Man, Paul, 1, 20, 109, 116
Derrida, Jacques, 33
de Vega, Lope, 116
Dickens, Charles, 47
discourse: definition of, 7–8; "news/nov-
  el," 12
documentary fiction: and "Cretan Liar"
  paradox, 123, 124, 125, 149n22; *see
  also* Poniatowska, Elena; *Hasta no verte,
  Jesús mío; La noche de Tlatelolco*
Donoso, José, 7
Dos Passos, John, 103, 117
Dumas *père,* Alexandre, 47
Dutaq, Armand, 46

Echeverría, Esteban, 4
"El acercamiento a Almotásim" ("The
  Approach to Almotasim"; Jorge Luis
  Borges), 106

Mariátegui, José Carlos, 62–3
Mármol, José, 17
Martí, José, 20, 84, 87, 88, 98, 99, 102, 127; as chronicler, 90–3, 144*n*7; and oratory, 92
Matto de Turner, Clorinda, 81
melodrama: definition of, 53; *see also Facundo, o Civilización y barbarie*
Michelet, Jules, 81
Miller, D. A., 42, 57, 58–9
Miller, J. Hillis, 18, 101
Modernism, Spanish American, 102, 127–8; and journalism, 17–18, 85–90, 110; and philology, 84–6; reevaluation of, 83–4
Modernist chronicles, 7, 121, 128; definition of, 84
Modernity: definition of, 2; and journalism, 13, 14, 15, 16, 17, 19, 108; and literature, 4, 19; and postmodernity, 2; and Sarmiento's journalism, 46; and Spanish America, 2–4; and violence, 3; and writing, 3–4
"Modesty of History, The" (Jorge Luis Borges), 107

narrative fiction: vs. journalism, studies of, 6–7; and literature, 6; *see also* journalism
Nervo, Amado, 84
Newgate novels, 57; *see also* crime story
news, *see* journalism
Nietzsche, Friedrich, 41, 79, 81, 82, 107

Oedipus Rex (Sophocles), 45, 140*n*1

Pacheco, José Emilio, 2
Paine, Thomas, 40
Palma, Ricardo, 17, 41, 62–82, 101, 110, 112, 126, 144*n*17
Payno, Manuel, 17, 121
Paz, Octavio, 2, 84, 100, 123, 126
Pérez Bonalde, Juan Antonio, 87
Pérez Galdós, Benito, 66, 79
Philp, Mark, 7
"Pierre Menard, Author of the *Quixote*" (Jorge Luis Borges), 106–7
Poggioli, Renato, 103
Poniatowska, Elena, 2, 20, 100, 111, 121–5, 129
Porras Barrenechea, Raúl, 70–1
Puig, Manuel, 100

Renan, Ernest, 84, 85

Rodríguez Freyle, Juan, 44
Rojas y Cañas, Ramón, 71–2
romances de ciego, see crime story
roman-feuilleton, see folletín
Rosas, Juan Manuel de, 42, 49–50, 51, 57, 58, 59–60, 61, 126, 127

Saco, José Antonio, 4
Sarduy, Severo, 21, 100
Sarmiento, Domingo Faustino, 3, 17, 41, 42–61, 93, 101, 126–7
Sartre, Jean-Paul, 117; *see also* Vargas Llosa, Mario
Schulman, Iván A., 84
sensationalism: definition of, 43–5; *see also Facundo, o Civilización y barbarie*
Shattuck, Roger, 103
Sigüenza y Góngora, Carlos, 40
Sophocles, 45
Stephens, Mitchell, 11, 43, 44, 131*n*7
Sue, Eugene, 46, 47

Taine, Hyppolite, 85
Tapia y Rivera, Alejandro, 121
Tiananmen Square, 1–2
Tlatelolco massacre, 1–2
Todorov, Tzvetan, 4, 5
Tradiciones peruanas (Ricardo Palma), 17, 20, 41, 102, 110, 112, 121, 126; allusions to journalism in, 67; Devil in, 76–9, 142*n*11; and *fait-divers*, 63, 73–8; and genealogy, 63, 79–81, 143*n*14; and genre, 63–6; orality in, 65–6; and Romantic populism, 62–3; and satirical journalism, 63, 69–73, 78, 142*n*9

Ucelay Da Cal, Margarita, 78
Usigli, Rodolfo, 126

Vallejo, César, 99
Vanguardism, *see* avant-garde
Vargas Llosa, Mario, 100, 110, 111, 117–21, 124, 125, 129; comments on Flaubert and Sartre, 117, 148*n*17; views on journalists and journalism, 118–19
Villaverde, Cirilo, 4

Watt, Ian, 9
White, Hayden, 7, 73
Wolfe, Tom, 121
Wordsworth, William, 93–4, 141*n*1

Zola, Emile, 66, 79